KARMIC TRACES

BY ELIOT WEINBERGER

AUTHOR

Works on Paper (1986)
19 Ways of Looking at Wang Wei (1987)
Outside Stories (1992)
Written Reaction (1996)
Karmic Traces (2000)

EDITOR

Montemora (1975-1982)
Una antología de la poesía norteamericana desde 1950 (1992)
American Poetry Since 1950: Innovators & Outsiders (1993)
Sulfur 33: Into the Past (1993)
James Laughlin, *Ensayos fortuitos* (1995)

EDITOR/TRANSLATOR

Octavio Paz, *Eagle or Sun?* (1970; 1976)
Octavio Paz, *A Draft of Shadows* (1980)
Homero Aridjis, *Exaltation of Light* (1981)
Octavio Paz, *Selected Poems* (1984)
Jorge Luis Borges, *Seven Nights* (1984)
Octavio Paz, *Collected Poems 1957–1987* (1987)
Vicente Huidobro, *Altazor* (1988)
Octavio Paz, *A Tree Within* (1988)
Octavio Paz, *Sunstone* (1991)
Cecilia Vicuña, *Unravelling Words and the Weaving of Water* (1992)
Xavier Villaurrutia, *Nostalgia for Death* (1992)
Octavio Paz, *In Light of India* (1997)
Octavio Paz, *A Tale of Two Gardens* (1997)
Octavio Paz, *An Erotic Beyond: Sade* (1998)
Jorge Luis Borges, *Selected Non-Fictions* (1999)
Bei Dao, *Unlock* (2000)

KARMIC TRACES

1993–1999

ELIOT WEINBERGER

A NEW DIRECTIONS BOOK

Earlier versions of these essays appeared frequently in *Lettre International* (Germany), *Vuelta* (Mexico), and *Jacket* (www.jacket.zip.com.au). Others were first published in *Artes de México* (Mexico), *Cult* (Brazil), *Heat* (Australia), *La Jornada Semanal* (Mexico), *Lateral* (Spain), *Letra Internacional* (Spain), *Magyar Lettre Internationale* (Hungary), *El Malpensante* (Colombia), *Sibila* (Spain), and in the United States in *Boston Review*, *Global City Review*, *The Nation*, *New England Review*, *Seneca Review*, *Sulfur*, *Tin House*, and *The Village Voice Literary Supplement*. Some were broadcast on the "Books and Writing" program of ABC Radio (Australia).

"Karmic Traces" was written for the Jerusalem Poets' Festival (1995) and, in Spanish translation, was the accompanying text for a book of photographs by Nina Subin (*Rastros kármicos*, Ed. Artes de México, 2000). "MacDiarmid" was the introduction to the *Selected Poetry* of Hugh MacDiarmid (New Directions, 1993). "In the Zócalo," "Genuine Fakes," and "Naked Mole-Rats" were published in *Written Reaction* (Marsilio, 1996). "Ackerley's *Hindoo Holiday*" was the introduction to an edition published by New York Review Books in 2000 and also appeared in *The New York Review of Books*. "Jón, Ólaf's Son" was published as a limited-edition chapbook (Canopic Press, 2000).

Special thanks to Linsey Abrams, Nelson Ascher, Frank Berberich, John D'Agata, Stephen Donadio, Clayton Eshleman, Edwin Frank, Dirk Höfer, Ivor Indyk, Éva Karádi, Ramona Koval, John Leonard, J. McCullogh, Stephen Smith, Peter Torberg, and John Tranter.

Book design by Sylvia Frezzolini Severance
Manufactured in the United States of America
New Directions Books are printed on acid-free paper.
First published as New Directions Paperbook 908 in 2000
Published simultaneously in Canada by Penguin Books Canada Limited

Library of Congress Cataloging in Publication Data

Weinberger, Eliot.
  Karmic traces: 1993–1999 / Eliot Weinberger.
    p. cm. — (New Directions paperbook; 908)
  Includes bibliographical references.
  ISBN 0-8112-1456-7 (acid-free paper)
    I. Title.

PS3573.E3928 K37 2000
814'.54—dc21   00-029222

New Directions Books are published for James Laughlin
by New Directions Publishing Corporation,
80 Eighth Avenue, New York, NY 10011

SECOND PRINTING

CONTENTS

"There is no place for the past to take place
except right now"

—*Robert Duncan*

for N.S., A.D. & S.

I

PARADICE

Snæfellsnes Peninsula. Iceland has created the most perfect society on earth, one from which the rest of the world has nothing to learn. For its unlikely Utopia is the happy accident of a history and a geography that cannot be duplicated, or even emulated, elsewhere.

Outside of the South Pacific, no ethnic group so small has its own entirely independent nation-state. There are only 268,000 Icelanders, of whom 150,000 live in and around Reykjavík, the capital. The second largest city, Akureyri, known for its arts scene and night life—their Barcelona—has 14,000. In the rest of the country there are few people, and the treeless wilderness of volcanoes, waterfalls, strange rock formations, steaming lava fields, geysers, glaciers, and icebergs seems like the ends of the earth, as though one were crossing into Tibet and found the sea.

Nearly all the roads are sparsely traveled and unpaved, yet this is a modern Scandinavian country where everything works, and where the state protects its citizens from birth to death. There is no unemployment, no poverty and no conspicuous wealth; education is universal. Per capita book consumption and production is by far the highest in the world. They live longer than almost anyone else. There is no pollution: the entire country is geothermally heated.

It is non-violent: no army, no guns, little crime. Prisoners, except the dangerous, go home for holidays; small children walk in the city alone. For the last thousand years, Icelandic women have had rights that were long unimagined elsewhere, such as the ability to divorce and keep half the property. It was the first nation with a woman president, and is the only one with an all-women political party with seats in Parliament. The Icelanders invented the idea of a parliament.

Incredibly, it is a capitalist consumer society without excess. They have everything, but only one or two kinds of everything. They live without the bombarded frenzy of competing brands, the demands of consumer expertise, and the

3

attendant dread that one has made the wrong choice. The traditional occupations of the major exports—fishing and sheepherding—are now performed by only a fraction of the population. The rest of the tiny work force must fill all the roles of a modern society: ambassador, plumber, anesthesiologist, programmer, cellist, cop. There is one television station, one well-known film director, one Nobel Prize novelist, one international rock star. In Iceland, modern life is complete, but lived on the scale of the tribal.

Like a tribe, it is a society rooted in the archaic. They may be the only technological people on earth who could speak fluently with their ancestors from a thousand years ago: Icelandic has remained the same since it split from Old Norse, and its alphabet retains two runic letters that no one else uses. They are required by law to have traditional names, and follow the ancient system of first name plus father's or mother's name plus "son" or "daughter." The telephone book lists people by their first names, and they're all the same: Jóhann Magnússon, Magnus Jóhannsson, Gréta Jóhannsdóttir. They can differentiate one another because they *know* one another.

Islanders, they are self-absorbed. In the 13th century, they produced a vast body of literature, unlike anything in Europe, that was a meticulous description of themselves. These are the sagas: the tales not of heroes or gods, but of ordinary people: the actual settlers who had come to the uninhabited land two hundred years before. There are scores of sagas, all interlocking: the same stories are told from different points of view; a person mentioned in passing in one becomes the protagonist of another. It is an enormous "human comedy" of love, greed, rage, lust, marriages and property settlements, travels, revenge, funerals and festivals, meetings, abductions, prophetic dreams and strange coincidences, fish and sheep. Nearly everyone in Iceland is descended from these people, and they know the stories, and the stories of what happened in the generations since.

One travels through Iceland with *The Visitor's Key*, an extraordinary guidebook that follows every road in the country step by step, as though one were walking with the Keeper of Memories. Iceland has few notable buildings, museums, or monuments. What it has are hills and rivers and rocks, and each has a story the book recalls. Here was a stone bridge which collapsed behind an escaping convicted murderer, proving his innocence. Here lived a boy whose magical powers were such, he could wither grass. Here a man died of exposure in a snowstorm, not knowing he was a few yards from his house. It is said that two chests of silver are hidden somewhere on this hill. In this hot spring, a famous outlaw boiled his meat. A man was buried here because the horses carrying his body refused to take another step. Here a man who stole more sheep than he needed was slain by a twelve-year-old boy. This farm refused shelter to a traveling pregnant woman, and was buried in a landslide that night. Some people have seen a man walking by this cliff with his head under his arm. Here was the home of a clergyman who was honored abroad for his development of medicinal cod liver oil, and was also known for having kidnapped his bride. Here lived a popular postman in the 18th century.

What other modern society so fully inhabits the landscape it lives in? Where else does the middle class still remember?

Sir Richard Burton, after the tropics and the deserts, was appalled by it. William Morris learned the language and translated some sagas, but preferred his reading to his two visits. Jules Verne never came, but placed the entrance to the center of the earth at the Snæfellsjökull volcano. Trollope came, late in life, and wrote a jolly account of huge meals and pretty women, but was shocked to find no bank. Here the young Auden, just before the war in Spain, wrote his strangest book.

They bake bread by putting it in the ground; they prefer their shark meat rotten. The use of pesticides is unknown among them. Nearly all the women have their first child before marriage. They allow no dogs in the capital. Their eyes are the exact pale blue shade of an iceberg. They believe in Hidden People. Their horses grow long coats in the winter, and sleep lying down. I have never seen so many kinds of moss.

[1996]

INDRIÐI INDRIÐASON

In 1903, Einar G. Hjörleifsson, a journalist and newspaper editor in the small northern town of Akureyri, Iceland's second largest city, read a review in a foreign magazine of F.W.H. Myers' scholarly exposition of spiritualism, *Human Personality and Its Survival of Bodily Death*, and asked the county supervisor to try to obtain a copy for the local library. Before the book arrived many months later, Hjörleifsson had already written articles in its defense, and had attempted a few seances that produced no results. The following year, he moved to the capital, Reykjavík, and changed his name to Einar Kvaran—a pseudonym that prefigures B. Traven and Arthur Cravan—under which he would later become a nationally famous writer of, unexpectedly, realist novels.

The sittings continued with some like-minded enthusiasts. At one, the group became excited when a young woman wrote automatically about the death of a relative on a sheep farm in "West World," the colony in Manitoba where a fourth of the population had emigrated after decades of famine. Weeks later, the news arrived that the relative was alive and well.

Disappointed, the group was at the point of disbanding when a printer's apprentice, Indriði Indriðason, twenty-two, raised without schooling on a distant croft, accidentally happened to attend a meeting. He had barely sat down when the table around which they had gathered began to shake violently. Indriði, in terror, ran out of the room. He was taken to Kvaran's house, where a table trembled, moved across the floor, and flipped over.

Kvaran encouraged the reluctant Indriði, and the printer's apprentice first fell into a trance shortly before Easter, 1905, and began writing automatically. He saw shadowy beings and swore at them; he saw himself as two identical people, linked by a cord. He became afflicted with headaches, insomnia, and depression, and resolved to go to "West World." Just before leaving, he fell ill: in his delirium, he saw a man with a gray beard operating on him. The man dictated a letter to Indriði which was given to Kvaran. If a group were to be formed, and certain instructions followed—these are not now known—greater things would be seen.

Kvaran founded the Experimental Society in the fall of 1905 and gathered prominent citizens: theologians, writers, a future Prime Minister, a Supreme Court judge, a member of Parliament. At the first meeting, the table suddenly lifted and banged into the chins of the assembled. Three men tried to push it down and could not. Indriði was not touching it. At the next session, a "control" appeared, who spoke through Indriði in his trance state and instructed the group to meet every night.

Knocks were heard at the third meeting, on the walls and on the ceiling. At the next, clicks were heard in the air, like fingers snapping, moving around the room, though Indriði was motionless. Still later, lights flashed in the dark room, some white, some red, of different sizes and shapes; fifty-eight in all were counted. There was no equipment available in Iceland at the time that could produce such flashes. One night, Indriði described a major fire in Copenhagen. When the Danish papers arrived a month later, the information was proved correct.

In November, Indriði began to levitate. In the darkness of the meetings, it was difficult to see, but the sitters heard him bumping against the ceiling, crashing to the floor, smashing furniture as he came down. Once, a match was lit, and Indriði was seen, horizontal, with his head on a table and nothing else to support him.

On December 6, a man appeared in a pool of light, with his back turned to the group. Indriði was in the corner, screaming. Strong gusts of wind blew through the room, disheveling hair and flipping the pages of books. Two weeks later, in the longest night of the sunless winter, Indriði, in his trance, suddenly shouted: "What are you going to do with those knives? No, no, no!" His left arm vanished. Seven sitters examined him, lit matches, and then lamps, but his arm could not be found. A half-hour later, it reappeared.

After a few consecutive evenings where the disappearance of his arm was repeated, Indriði became ill, and the meet-

ings were suspended. They resumed in the darkness of the
winter of 1906–7, when the seance room would become filled
with a blinding white light. In the light a human would
appear, dressed in a long white robe, speaking Danish with a
heavy Copenhagen accent, and calling himself Mr. Jensen. He
would appear repeatedly, for a few seconds at a time, in different parts of the room, sometimes standing behind Indriði's
chair. At one meeting, forty witnesses saw him, including the
Bishop of Iceland, the Magistrate of Reykjavík, and the British
Consul. The Bishop insisted that further meetings be held at
his own house, where, surprisingly, the appearances of Mr.
Jensen became more frequent and the light more intense.

In September 1907, Indriði went to visit a clergyman in the
Westman Islands, where people lived on smoked fish and
smoked puffin. There, he met an unpleasant apparition
named Jón, described as a man in his shirt-sleeves, and trou-
bles began.

On December 7, Indriði and his roommate, a theology student named Þórður, were sleeping in their house when a plate
was thrown on the floor and Indriði's bed moved from the
wall. The next night, Kvaran stayed with them; the doors were
locked and a lamp was kept burning. Shoes began to be tossed
around the room; then the head and foot of the bed alternate-
ly lifted and crashed down. A boot smashed the lamp, and
Indriði screamed that he was being dragged. He was pulled
headfirst out of the room, while the two men tugged at his
ankles. They finally managed to get him back on the bed,
where Indriði's legs were lifted up and the men could not
force them down.

On the 10th, a man named Brynjólfur stayed with Indriði
and Þórður. Candlesticks fell on the floor, and a hairbrush
flew across the air. Indriði cried out that Jón was there.
Brynjólfur lay down on top of Indriði on his bed, and the table
next to them floated up and landed on them. After a period of
quiet, Brynjólfur went back to bed. Indriði screamed that Jón
was back. Water from a water basin was thrown in
Brynjólfur's face and a chamber pot sailed across the room.
Brynjólfur again lay down on top of Indriði, and the bed
moved from the wall. He was holding Indriði down as best he

could, while a table rose and was banging him on the head.
The men decided to leave the house, and began to get dressed.
Indriði stood up and was thrown back on the bed. A bowl flew
through the air, changed direction, and splintered against a
wall. Indriði screamed again, and Brynjólfur and Þórður saw
him suspended horizontally. Both men tried to push him
down, and they too were lifted into the air, as chairs, cushions,
water basins and water bottles were flung and smashed
against the walls.

In a country with months of near-total darkness: where the
language recognized twenty-seven different kinds of ghosts:
where everyone knew, from the sagas, the gossip of their
ancestors of a thousand years before, and all who had come
and gone since: where so much of the population was living
and dying a world away to the west: on an island that was still
a Danish colonial outpost, that until recently had not a single
road across its eerie treeless landscape: where electricity was
new to the city: where most of the population lived in remote
settlements and spent the winters telling stories to each other,
packed into tiny rooms in peat-covered cottages heated by the
warmth of the animals and their own bodies: Indriði became
a celebrity, the most famous Icelander of his time.
    The Experimental Society built a special house where he
could live and work, with a seance room that could hold a
hundred people, a large crowd in the minuscule city. The popularity of the seances, ridiculed in the local press, attracted the
attention of Iceland's most honored scientist, Guðmundur
Hannesson, founder of the Icelandic Scientific Society, twice
President of the University of Iceland, Reykjavík City Council
member, and leading light in both the Icelandic and Danish
Associations of Physicians. Guðmundur decided to expose
Indriði by subjecting the gatherings to scientific methods of
verification.
    The hall was sealed, and a man directed to hold Indriði's
hands throughout the session. A megaphone on an iron stand
rose from a table and a voice spoke through it into
Guðmundur's ear. A heavy music box flew through the air
playing a melody. A table turned upside-down and a bench

was dragged; loose objects careened. There were knocks and voices.

Guðmundur next inspected the ceiling and floor for hidden compartments. He constructed a net, stretched tight and nailed to the room on all sides, to serve as a barrier between Indriði and the audience. All possible apertures and crevices were checked and sealed, and movable objects placed out of Indriði's reach. Guðmundur reported: "It was the same as at the previous seance: everything went mad and tumbled about. It was even noisier than it was on the previous occasion."

For the third meeting, the examination of the room was even more thorough, and Indriði was undressed and searched. Only two people besides Guðmundur, Indriði, and his "watchman" were allowed to attend. Guðmundur wrote: "This is no joke. It is a life-and-death struggle for sound reason and one's own conviction against the most execrable form of idiocy and superstition." At the seance objects flew. The chair was pulled out from under Indriði and smashed. Guðmundur, standing away from the others, was struck hard in the back, as though by a closed fist. Indriði was pulled feet first toward the ceiling as the "watchman" tried to haul him down. Voices of different kinds and with different accents were heard cursing; the sitters' chairs were pulled from them. A lectern firmly nailed to the floor was torn loose, and Indriði and the "watchman" were dragged about. Broken glass and trash were thrown in Guðmundur's face from a direction where no one was present. Surveying the rubble of the room, Guðmundur concluded that "there is no possibility of explaining" what had happened.

Guðmundur attended twenty more seances, each time inventing stricter controls: The meetings were moved to other houses, the location announced only minutes before, with guards stationed outside. Indriði was undressed and put into a kind of straitjacket to keep him from moving. Phosphorescent tape was ordered from Europe and placed on Indriði and various objects to observe their movements. The phenomena were repeated: flying objects; levitation; winds blowing from nowhere; varied voices in Icelandic, French,

Danish, and Swedish, some speaking simultaneously, often cursing; invisible punches; furniture being smashed, the megaphone and the music box swinging wildly over the heads of the audience. A woman's voice, musically trained, was heard singing when no women were present. Once, the room filled with fog.

Guðmundur published his findings in scientific journals. He wrote: "It is my firm conviction that the phenomena are unquestionable realities."

In the summer of 1909, Indriði went to visit his parents with his recent fiancée. They both caught typhoid, and she died. Too weak to continue, he never held another seance. He married another woman, and they had a daughter who died in infancy. Indriði contracted tuberculosis and died in a sanatorium in 1912 at age twenty-nine.

[1997]

AN ARCHEOLOGY OF DREAMS

[The North, c. 1000]

Þorbjörg of Indriðastaðir dreamed that eighty wolves passed by with flames coming from their mouths, and among them was a white bear.

Glaumvör dreamed that a bloody sword was sticking out from her husband's tunic, and that a river ran through the house, sweeping away all their things.

Hersteinn Blund-Ketilsson dreamed he saw his father on fire.

Ásmundr Kappabani dreamed that a group of women stood over him, holding weapons, and said: "You are expected to be a leader, yet you fear eleven men."

King Gormr dreamed that three black oxen came out of the sea, ate the grass down to the roots, and went back to the sea. Then he heard a great crash.

Bárðr dreamed that a giant tree grew from his father's hearth, covered with blossoms, and that one of the branches was solid gold.

Gísli dreamed he went to a house, filled with friends and relatives, and they sat by seven fires, some flaming brightly and some nearly burnt out. He dreamed that a woman came to him on a gray horse and invited him to her house; they rode together, and went inside, and there were soft cushions on the seats. Then he dreamed that another woman came, and washed his head in blood.

Blindr dreamed he saw King Haddingr's falcon with all its feathers plucked out.

Guðrún dreamed she was wearing an ugly hat; she wanted to take it off, but people told her not to, so she pulled it off her head and threw it in a brook. She dreamed she was standing by a lake, wearing a silver ring on her arm which slipped off into the water. She dreamed she was wearing a gold ring on her arm which slipped off, hit a rock, broke into pieces, and the pieces began to bleed. She dreamed she was wearing a gold helmet, set with precious stones, and that it was so heavy she could not walk.

Kostbera dreamed that the sheets of her husband's bed were on fire.

Þorkell Eyjólfsson dreamed his beard was so large it covered the land.

Þorgils Örrasbeinsstjúpr dreamed he looked at his knee, and five leeks were growing out of it.

Þorgils Böðvarsson dreamed that a tall woman came to his door, wearing a child's cloak, and she was very sad.

Hálfdan dreamed he had hair more beautiful than anyone, that it grew in all colors and all lengths: some fell down to his knees, some to his hips, some to his shoulders, and some were merely tufts.

Ragnhildr dreamed she took a thorn out of her smock and it grew from her hand into a great tree that was red at the bottom, green in the middle, and snow-white at the top.

Þorsteinn Surtr dreamed he was awake but everyone else was asleep; then he dreamed he fell asleep and everyone else woke up.

Þorsteinn Uxafótr dreamed that a burial mound opened and a man dressed in red came out. He greeted him pleasantly and invited him into his house. They descended into the mound, which was well furnished. On his right he saw eleven men, sitting on a bench, dressed in red. On his left he saw twelve men, sitting on a bench, dressed in blue.

King Sverrir dreamed that a man came to his bed and told him to follow. They walked out of town and into the countryside, where they came to a fire on which a man was being roasted. The guide told him to sit and eat, and gave him a roasted human leg. He ate reluctantly, but with each bite he enjoyed it more, and couldn't stop eating.

Jón, bishop of Hólar, dreamed that he was praying before a large crucifix, that Jesus bent down and whispered something in his ear, but he did not understand the words.

Þuríðr Þorkelsdóttir dreamed that her dead husband appeared and told her not to think ill of her son-in-law.

Flosi dreamed that he and his friends were in Lómagnúpr, looking at the mountain. Then the peak opened, and a man came out, wearing a goatskin jacket and carrying an iron staff. He called each of the men by his name. Flosi asked him what the news was, and the man told him there wasn't any.

Án the Black dreamed that a repulsive woman appeared by his bed, cut out his entrails, and stuffed his body with brushwood. Then he dreamed that she took out the brushwood and put his entrails back.

Þórhaddr Hálfjótsson dreamed his tongue was so long it wound around his neck.

Sturla Sighvatsson told his friend that he had dreamed that he had a sausage in his hand, that he had straightened it out, broken it in half with his hands, and given half to this same friend. Moreover, he knew that the dream was occurring now, in the same moment of time in which he was telling the dream to his friend, holding a sausage in his hand.

King Atli dreamed that the reeds he wanted to grow were torn
up by the roots, reddened in blood, brought to his table, and
given him to eat. He dreamed he ate the hearts of hawks, with
honey.

A man from Skagafjörðr dreamed he came into a great house
where two women were rocking. They were covered with
blood, and blood rained on the windows.

Þorleifr Þorgilsson dreamed his sister gave him a piece of
cheese, and that all the crust was cut off it.

[1998]

JÓN, ÓLAF'S SON

1.

Friends! God kept his hand over Jón, Ólaf's son, in the air, on the earth, in the waters, on the ocean floor, in fire, in sleeping and waking, under a burning sky and a cold one, near to the mother-country and far, among Christians and heathens, in prosperity and adversity. These things did not happen that they might be forgotten.

Ólaf, Jón's son, of Álftafjördur in the parish of Eyri, Iceland, a man of some mark but no great wealth, and Ólöf, Þorsteinn's daughter, had fourteen children, of whom three survived childhood. Þóra was three years older than Halldór, who was fourteen years older than Jón, born on the Sunday after All Saints, November 4, 1593, in a driving snow that delayed his baptism.

Jón, Ólaf's son, was in good health for two years, then became a sickly child, prone to accidents. At five, he nearly drowned in a brook, pretending his cradle was a boat. At eight, Halldór rescued him from the Fjarðará salmon river. That same year, he and his horse miscalculated the tide and were washed out to sea, barely able to swim back. Jón's mother greatly feared the rivers, but others said it would be his lot to travel across the waters.

In his seventh year there was a plague of the flux, and his father, Ólaf, Jón's son, died. Halldór took charge of the farm and married Randíður, Ólaf's daughter, and had six children. His eighth year was the winter called The Great Torture: many died of disease and hunger, many sheep were lost, but below the fold at Hattardal, a whale came up out of the ice to provide sustenance for all.

That was the winter when Jón, Þorleif's son, the minister at Staður in the Snæfell district, sent his son to rescue the sheep from a dangerous place, and the son never returned, but did much damage as a ghost. He enjoyed his meals as if he were alive, and would throw stones from the mountain at those who would not give him food. Someone saw him eating dried fish and offered him a knife, but he replied: "The dead need no knife: they stand and rend."

That was the time when a woman named Bóthildur went over the pass to Önundarfjörður with her son Ketill, who was two. A black fog descended, and she went astray toward a place called Valagil, beset by precipices, and on the edge of those cliffs, exhausted from carrying her child, fell asleep in the Lord. For days men heard a strange howling in the mountains, and all the farmers liable to taxation assembled, armed with their three-spiked halberds, to search for that strange beast or ghost. They found the woman long dead and her infant son, alive, guarding the body. The boy was taken in, grew up in the district, became a laborer, and died at twenty.

At fourteen, Jón's ill health ended thanks to God and a Danish ship's captain named Anders who sent an apple to Jón's mother. Jón ate the half of it and prospered thereafter.

At his age twenty-two, in the spring, just before Crossmass, an English ship was thrown off course in a storm and moored in the fishing place called the City of Rome. Although it was forbidden, Jón rowed out to see the ship, met the captain, an upright man, and undertook to voyage to foreign parts with him. His mother had long expected this, and her grief was not as bitter as it might have been. Jón took, to sell abroad, 200 salted cod; a barrel of train-oil, made from sharks and seals, worth 190 fish; two full chests, and two lengths of homespun.

A violent storm off Ísafjörður, where he lost his barrel of oil. At Laugardalsstaður, the minister came aboard and urged him not to go. A southeast gale off the Horn. The Faroes, which he couldn't see. Shetland, an island inhabited by poor folk. Seven hundred herring-boats in the shallows around the Orkneys. A man named Reuben: the first time Jón saw a man

smoke tobacco. After seven weeks, the place in England called
Newcastle, where three hundred ships left the harbor laden
with coal; two were lost in a gale that night. Yarmouth, where
the church had eight bells. Then Harwich, where the ship was
bound.

In Harwich, a rich man named Simon Cook invited Jón to dinner. He sent four men to accompany him and told him to fill
his hat with stones, for the roads were full of highwaymen
and murderers. The first mate took him to the inn owned by a
man named Thomas Twidd, who had an excellent wife,
Bersheba, whom he treated ill, and a pretty and taking daughter named Temperance. Twidd feigned amazement at Jón's
good English in such short a time; the first mate, to spite the
captain, arranged for Jón to be hired as a servant; Twidd
stored Jón's goods for safekeeping, and sent him on an errand
back to Newcastle for a month. When he came back the goods
were gone; Twidd threw a plate at Jón's head and instructed
his boy to beat him and drive him out.

Jón heard that a Danish ship sent by the King with gifts for
King James had arrived in London, and he sailed there to seek
a post, losing his good hat on the way. There were swans on the
river, called the King's birds, and it was death to any man who
harmed them. Jón lent his suit and prayer book to a Dutchman
who wanted to attend church and was never seen again. The
city was so vast that compasses were placed at regular intervals
in the streets, that the people might find their way.

He sailed to Denmark on the ship *St. Peter*, and on the voyage
befriended two men: Magnus, a Norwegian who was the
Danish King's groom, and Jakob, who had spent seven years
in London learning the weaving of gold and silver threads
they call *passementerie*. Magnus hired Jón as his under-groom,
and he worked at the King's stables by the High Bridge in
Copenhagen, currying and dressing down the horses, water-
ing and exercising them, and loudly beating drums around
them so that they would be accustomed to the sounds of war.

The King summoned Magnus to his court in Jutland. One night, returning to his lodging, and not knowing the town, Magnus knocked long and loudly at the wrong door. One of the King's guards rushed out with his halberd and killed him. Because of that deed, the guard lost his head and Jón had lost his job.

There was a chance for work in the King's cellar, then a post assisting the Steward of the King's Plate, but a pewterer named Rasmus persuaded Jón to join the King's Artillery, and he took the oath on the salt and bread that signifies Christ and His Word.

Jón served on the night watch at the Arsenal: a captain of the guard, a piper, a drummer, and twenty-four men. They assembled in a circle, and the captain whispered the night's password to the man on his right, who in turn whispered it to the next, until it reached the captain again. If the word had changed, they went around the circle again.

One morning Jón was walking by the iron grating of the Church of the Blessed Virgin. A man and woman were ahead of him, on the way to fetch water from the well there. When they looked into the well they cried out: a dead baby girl was floating in it. Five hundred servant girls were summoned by the authorities and examined to see if their breasts had milk. It was not so with any of them, but there were rumors that the child had come from the house of a very learned person, the Honorable Mr. M.

Then two misshapen children were born on Drivers' Street, and at their funeral the minister Master Menelaus preached against the abuses prevalent in the city, the forbidden extravagances and the scandalous new fashions in women's dress, for the deformities of these two baby girls had the appearance of hair-braids, peaked caps, high furbelows on the shoulders, fringed petticoats, and high-heeled shoes.

Farmers came to the city on market days with rye, malt, barley, three kinds of groats, wheat, hops, honey, butter, cheese, swine, geese, ducks, and many kinds of freshwater fish. They were required to leave the city by noon, lest they spend their earnings on ale, and small boys would pelt them with horse dung as they drove their wagons out.

Three witches were discovered and burnt. Two boys, aged seven and nine, fell into a fight outside their schoolroom, and the younger killed the elder with his knife. The gates to the city were closed and no boys under ten allowed to leave, but the boy escaped. It was said that a ferryman named Jens turned into a wolf, against his will, on certain nights. A kindly minister, Master Søren, eighty-five years old, asked his servant to chop wood for the Sunday meal. He sent one of his two serving girls to give the man some ale, and the man split her skull with the axe. The minister sent the second girl to find the first, and she met the same end. Then the man entered the house, killed the minister and his wife and stole off with their goods. Three years later, the minister's nephew saw a man wearing his uncle's hat at an inn in Holstein, and the man was seized.

An evil man appeared in the dream of a poor cobbler and led him to the St. Nicholas Church and showed him where to find the alms-box, which he stole. It was a fortune in small coins, some three hundred rixdollars, each one worth forty-five codfish. The man spent extravagantly and was soon discovered.

The King's Chancellor, who was almost eighty, took ill while dining with the King and died. His wife did not believe the account of his death, and afterwards strange things happened. The King was preparing to sail on the ship *Caritas* when a sudden storm rose from the east and all the King's provisions were lost. It took many weeks to refurbish the ship, which the King renamed *Patientia*. He sailed out on that ship in good weather, but hit a violent gale off the island of Amager, and the mainmast, nine tree-trunks thick, cracked and twelve men fell off the main-top. Then, harbored at Bremerholm at Easter, with netting around the bulwarks and flags and pennants on the mast-tops and yardarms, the chaplain was delivering a

sermon when a double-bottomed barrel drifted by. The man
on watch caught it with his hook and brought it on board;
inside was a headless corpse. For many weeks, nine men—Jón
among them—felt the presence of a ghost. But the King
returned safely, and at the news of his arrival in Copenhagen,
the Chancellor's wife withdrew to her bedchamber and died.

Jón's mother sent him 740 fish from Iceland with an honest
man, but the man died of the plague in Hamburg and Jón
never recovered his fish. He defended a friend's wife against
the advances of a man named Morten the Mouthstrong, who
plunged a knife in his shoulder; Master Jakob the doctor told
Jón he had lost three pints of articulated humors. Years later,
this same Morten stabbed a man on a ship off the coast of
Spain and, in accord with the naval laws, was lashed to the
dead man and thrown overboard. On that same voyage, a
Norwegian named Olaf was stabbed by a Spaniard; the winter before, Olaf, for no reason, had smashed a tankard on Jón's
head.

Jón got drunk with a student named Finn and fell into an open
smack that was tied at the quay, which led to a brawl with the
citizens on the night watch, and broken teeth and broken
bones. The next night they all got together over ale to laugh
about it, and Jón was in another fight with a mason who
insulted Iceland.

He saw jugglers walking on wooden stilts as tall as a house.
He saw a man dance on a rope stretched from the tower of the
cathedral to the tower of the town hall. He saw actors who
performed comedies full of adventure, and each wore different clothes according to his part in the story. He saw a surgeon
who could heal a stab wound in twelve hours. He saw a den-
tist who had cured the daughters of kings, who rubbed an
ointment on a bad tooth and a moment later the tooth was
spat out. He helped a master craftsman from Italy make a clay
mold as tall as himself, working all night, and when the mold
was finished the craftsman insisted they both pray. The
bronze was not quite ready to be poured, but the King came

by and insisted it was ready and turned the cock on the channel himself and then rode off. The craftsman, wishing he were
dead, swore at Jón that he hadn't prayed hard enough. When
the bronze cooled, they smashed the mold and there before
them was a boy with flowing hair riding a long-necked swan
and a maiden beside him with luxuriant curling tresses, but
her left breast was missing.

A member of the High Council had a cook named Herman
who fell ill one day. He left the house dressed in dark clothing,
but came back dressed in red, for he had become a lunatic. He
attacked his master and lady with a sword, but was subdued
before he could cause harm. Jón was summoned to watch
over the cook as he slept, and he spent the night reading about
Eternal Death and the unspeakable martyrdoms and tortures
prepared in Hell for the Devil, his Angels, and the Damned.
The book was called *The Divine High Court of Justice*, and in the
morning Herman was well again.

Jón was sent to Kronborg Castle in Elsinore for two years, as
one of thirty gunners. Every third night he would serve on the
watch of fifty men: ten gunners and forty soldiers. They
would line up for duty in the late afternoon, and the sergeant
would review the ranks and hand over those who were drunk
to the turnkey. That winter the sound froze over, and it was
the custom that when the farmers could drive their wagons
across the sound, their goods were not taxed at the market.
That was the year, 1618, when a comet was seen across the sky,
and the next year it brought the plague.

The King and the King of Sweden signed a treaty and it
became strictly forbidden, in public or private, in speech or
song, to speak ill of the Swedes.

Jón was assigned to the ship *Victor* to sail north in search of the
remaining cohorts of the notorious pirate, Mendoza, who had
lately been captured and hanged in Copenhagen. The island
of Vardø, where there had been trouble with the Finns, who
were addicted to magical practices; eighty men and women

had been executed for trolldom. Northeast across the White Sea, which was the color of milk, into Russia, but no pirates were found. Russians came on board bearing freshly split salmon on painted trays. Jón was told that there are many large towns in that vast land of Russia, but that all the houses are made of wood. When someone dies, the dead body is placed on one side of a large scale, and a wooden statue, its size according with the person's age, is placed on the other side. If the statue is heavier than the body, the person's soul is saved; but if the body is heavier, the soul is damned. They eat hard salted fare and drink brandy as if it were water and swallow a pint and a half with a single gulp.

Finns came aboard at Hálogaland, dressed in the skins of reindeer, which they decorated with colored cloth cut into the shapes of stars and flowers, with strips of colored cloth on their caps and on their shoes. Their women wore much gold and silver in their ears, and forehead bands, and coral bracelets. They were much addicted to butter and fat, which they drank like ale with their meals.

It was decided that the *Victor* and the five ships with it would sail to Iceland to help the people against the Spanish pirates who had been marauding the land. But off the coast of Eyjafjall a storm rose that lasted a fortnight, and the ship was blown to the Faroe Islands; Jón could not set foot on his homeland again. The men thought that the storm had been brought on by magic: that the Icelanders had mistaken the sudden appearance of the six ships and thought they too were pirates.

In a fortnight in the Faroes, Jón drank three kinds of mead, many kinds of wine, Hamburg ale, Lünbeck ale, Rostock ale, Trondheim ale, two kinds of Copenhagen ale, and three kinds of English ale. On the ship the *Unicorn* a ship's mate was hanged from the bowsprit for the crime of laziness: in the midst of the great storm, he had relieved himself in the room where bread is stored. Twenty-two men on the ships were sick with scurvy, but none died, save one, a Norwegian. In the feasts with the Faroese, many shots were fired from the ships.

On shore, a woman was milking her cow when a cannon ball
flew by, startling the cow who knocked over the milk, causing
the woman to faint. The next day she took the cannon ball and
rowed out to the ship to demand recompense. On their return
to Denmark, each man was welcomed according to the friends
he possessed.

Twenty-four men from the country of the Biscayans came to
Copenhagen to hunt whales. They were sent out on four
ships, Jón on one of them, that shared the voyage to
Greenland with two more, the *Unicorn* and the *Lamprey*, under
the command of Jens Munk, who was learned in navigation
and the movements of the stars. His mother had been an
unfreewoman and his father a naval hero who was thrown
into prison, committed suicide there, and was buried beneath
the gallows. Munk was searching for the Northwest Passage,
and of the sixty-six men on the two ships, only he and two
others returned.

Along the Greenland coast, the whalers came across the shack
where an Englishman had spent an entire year alone, the
result of a drunken wager. When the ship came to retrieve
him, they found three dead polar bears near the shack that he
had shot through the window. The sailors thought he was
dead, but then they heard a voice singing: a poem of a hundred stanzas the man had composed through the long winter.

Four whales were boiled down to 1,500 barrels of oil. Twenty-
two reindeer were caught; three would make up a barrel of
meat. A polar bear came into the camp, and the Biscayans harpooned him, presenting the Admiral with its skin and a large
feast for all. The tail of a harpooned troll-whale flipped the
whaler's zeluper, but they all were swimmers and none were
lost. By August, the ship was caked in ice, though the sun was
still shining; at night Jón stood watch waist-deep in snow.

Days of storm off the Norwegian coast separated the ships,
and Jón's ship drifted without sails on the North Sea, unable
to see beyond the giant swells, and lost its gilt figurehead. The

Admiral was weeping, and the sailors put all their money into the box for the poor. By the time they reached land, half of the men were immobile with scurvy, their teeth coming loose. Jón taught them to rub salt on their gums until they bled, and then rub tobacco ash into the wounds, which cured but was painful to endure. The voyage was four months and fifteen had died.

Jón returned to his post as a guard, the only Icelander in the King's service, but the Chief Master of the Arsenal, a man named Grabow, held a grudge against him, and contrived that Jón be charged with missing his watch. Jón was lowered on a hempen rope into the vaulted dungeon of the Blue Tower. His only companion for a while was a farmer who, on a Wednesday, had delivered a load of the King's firewood that was due on Tuesday. Lies were told by Grabow and others at Jón's trial, and he was sentenced to death.

A secret appeal to the King; the sentence commuted; but Jón was sent to Bremerholm prison and made to wear an iron ring around his neck with a large bell. His cellmate was the chief apprentice of a tower-builder and deranged of mind, who would sit reading books, then fling them across the room, cursing God, then weep and repent. Jón prayed against the devil within the apprentice, and he was saved. Released from prison, the apprentice replaced his master, who had recently died, and became the widow's husband. Jón wore his bell until the King visited and restored his freedom.

There was more to the story of Grabow, Jón's enemy. A woman named Mette had tricked many farmers by claiming to be skilled in the healing arts. She would measure with a band those who had the wasting sickness, and make signs and passes over them; she said she knew cures for colic and ague, and could put a stop to wet weather. Rumors reached the Castle and the Governor conceived a plan to trick her. His wife sent for Mette and told her that a silver jug was missing and asked her to discover the thief. The next morning Mette named a serving maid; the Governor stepped from behind a door and had her arrested. Mette was tortured in the Town

Hall but confessed to nothing. She said they should put to the
rack those women who kill their mates with poison, not her.
She told this story:

A woman named Anna, wife of Captain Peter Holst, a God-
fearing man of dignified appearance, had come to her to buy
as much poison as would suffice to kill a man. The boarder in
their house for ten years, the very same Grabow, the father of
two of her children, had pressed her once and for all to
remove the obstacle of her husband. After many entreaties
and much cash, Mette sold her the poison. Anna put it in a jug
of ale and asked the children's nurse to carry it up to her husband.

Anna and Grabow had also caused the death of a neighbor, a
pious weaver's wife, Elizabeth, who was the first to speak
publicly of their evil conduct toward the worthy old man
Peter Holst. They bribed two young men to give the woman a
fright, to stand under her window and make supernatural
screeching noises, as though demons were about. Elizabeth
was near her confinement, and at the sounds she fell down
dead.

Mette was put to death in the Gammeltorv, the usual place for
executions. The Burgomaster's men came for Anna, who
pulled a knife inlaid with silver from her pocket and plunged
it into her heart. The innocent and pious nurse was executed.
But Grabow, with powerful connections among the nobility,
went free.

Anna's coffin lay unburied for months in the New Graveyard,
where plague victims were sent and where one of the sextons
was known to dig up the newly buried, open the coffin, strike
the corpse, and command it to stand up. Danes held wakes of
great merrymaking, with food and drink, and this custom carried to the graveyards. Families would picnic there on
Sundays, and a sexton at the New Graveyard ran a tavern. Jón
would often go to rest his elbows on Anna's coffin and drink
a quart of ale.

Two ships were being outfitted for the voyage to the Indies: the *Christianshavn* and the *Pearl*, which had been built in Holland entirely of fir, and whose rudder, freshly cut with as yet no iron on it, could barely be carried by sixty men. Jón, weary of serving under Grabow, who was still his commander, signed on for a wage of thirteen gulden a month, 260 cod.

The night before the voyage, a handsome young man greeted Jón in the street and invited himself into Jón's lodging for a jug of ale. He said his name was Frederick, which Jón did not believe, and he said he had a certain gift. He spoke of many things, past and to come. He told the serving girl that she had secretly had a baby with the man she was to marry, and that he had deserted her. He told Jón he would marry twice, and have a child with the second wife. He described the good and bad qualities of Jón's character, and all were accurate. And he said that Jón would fall into great peril on the voyage, that God would deliver him from losing his life, but that he would bear the mark of it for as long as he lived. Then Frederick left, and it happened that Jón never saw him again.

2.

Eighty-eight men on the *Christianshavn*. Eight gunners, Jón among them. A sailmaker, a smith, a cook and his helper, a minister, three carpenters, a trumpeter, a doctor and his assistant, six merchants who were passengers. Three watches of seventeen men each. Sweeping the decks with hard brooms, lifting buckets of water from the gunwale to wash down the decks with hempen swabs, shaking out the gunpowder so it did not form lumps, turning over the sails, cleaning out the pumps. No swearing or ungodly talk at meals. No sleeping in wet woolen clothes, for they breed pink worms that get in the flesh. If a man pulled a knife on another man, that same knife would be used to pin his right hand to the mainmast. Morning and evening prayers.

Three days a week two pounds of meat each. Four days a week, two pounds of Kildin klipfish, which is beaten, soaked, and boiled. For each mess of seven men, one pound of butter for dipping per week, one quart measure of groats on fish days and one quart measure of peas or beans on meat days. Three and a half pounds of bread per week, measured out on Saturday. A mutchkin, one half-pint, of wine after dinner and supper. A three-pint can of ale every twenty-four hours until south of the Barbary Coast, where ale turns sour. Each man had to supply his own tobacco, cloves, nutmeg, caraway seeds, powdered and whole ginger, and brandy.

The first mate died on the second night out. England; the Channel; the Spanish Main: from there, 3,500 sea miles as the crow flies to India; the Barbary Coast. A miscalculation brought the ship too close to the headlands where man-eaters live; there they put men on iron grids and roast them for food. The land was smooth as an eggshell, with sands yellow and white, and little villages where crowds of people had gathered armed and in battle array as the ship sailed past, under the favoring wind called *tapass* or *masson*.

Eighteen weeks without sight of land. Alcorem, porbeagles, and dolphins caught with a seven-barbed spear attached to a harpoon; the dolphins cooked with a sauce made of honey or prunes, the porbeagles boiled in sharp salt and eaten with vinegar, though few have a taste for it. Duradd, caught on a hook with a three-cornered piece of red cloth attached, and good to eat. A boat floated out on a line behind the ship for the flying fish to flop into, sometimes as many as twelve at a time. The Captain shot two albatrosses, half as large again as a swan and visible from half a sea-mile away, thin but good to eat.

The sun-fish that rises to the surface and cannot go down again until the sun sets, large and awe-inspiring as it tosses in the waves, a gray-brown monster of the sea. The *slúkupp*, upright as a staff, a spout of water rising into the heavens from the ocean, caused by an opening in the sky; at the sight of it, a sea-mile away, the whole crew snatched the hats from their heads and fell to prayer.

New Year's, 1623, crossing Equinoctialis, the Equator line. There, on the spring and autumn equinoxes, all the winds blow out of the sky so that a ship cannot move for twelve or thirteen weeks, and men are smitten with strange diseases.

South of the line, the constellations are different and the phases of the moon look backwards. The water drawn up in buckets is so hot that a man could hardly hold his hand in it. The food that needs to be soaked free of salt turns black after an hour. The decks are so hot that one crosses them as though they were on fire; the pitch melts off and the ship glistens white. Worms called *teredos* burrow into the timber, and all vessels going to the Indies must have a skin of lead under the fir.

Land sighted at the Caput de Bona Sperantia, and the first man to see it was given a half-can of wine. On an island in the bay there were many seals, walking like men; Jón thought they were people. A bird called *pihvin* that had a seal's skin and a bird's form, that walked upright and could not fly.

Jón and his watch took a small boat to the island of *pihvins*, the first time he had walked on land in five months. It was hard to find footing, owing to the ordure of the seals and birds. On the highest point was a large post nailed with planks on which there were over a thousand initials or marks; the men added theirs. A huge whale lay at the bottom of a cliff where the seals were tossed in the heavy surf; it swallowed great numbers of seals and then vomited them; its bellowing was terrifying and the earth seemed to tremble at it. The chaplain fired many rounds at the whale, who ignored the bullets as if they were specks of dust. Three of the men flayed a living seal, then set it back in the surf, where its red suit caused much barking and commotion among the others.

Further up the coast they lay for two weeks to scour the hulls and repair the ship. The natives abandoned their nets and food and would not come visit. At night, the men could see great bonfires and crowds of people up on the mountain; some said they were signaling an invitation to come see them, some said it was to lure the men into a trap, and some thought these were sacrificial fires to their idols. Niels, a gunner, died and was buried, but a lion dug up the grave. The men wrote letters, and placed them in a box in a deep hole, with a sign above it—"Here lie letters which are to go to Denmark, from the ship *Christianshavn*"—in case a homeward bound ship should pass by.

Five weeks to Madagascar, a land fertile in everything that serves to maintain mankind: rice, cotton, sugar, lemons, cloves, ginger, saffron, and many other things. The people were black, smiling, mild-eyed, and had curly hair like the wool of young lambs; their lower lip drooped and their teeth were white; they would trade a cow for a scrap of iron. Their cows had a third horn on the ridge between the shoulders, but it was no real horn, for it was covered with hair and was nothing but fat inside, though the rest of the flesh was lean. They drank wine made from palm trees, which was very sweet, and grew a fruit called *banana*, which was delicious, as if there were fat in it, and hung in bunches the size of a guillemot, the seabird they hang to dry for fuel in Iceland.

A king's son came on board, wearing a gold web around his waist, set with jewels; a gold cloth on his head, adorned with more jewels; gold rings in his nostrils and on each finger and toe; and above his ankles large gold rings set with precious stones. All over his skin were printed pictures of animals and birds. He brought them palm wine and was merry.

Dense clouds black as coal that bring a storm beyond belief. Water comes from the air as though it were being poured; to drink it causes men to fall sick. Lightning and thunderclaps flit and roar about the ship, as if all heaven and earth were passing away, and none dare stand in the open. The masts bowed and bent; the ship on her side and almost capsized. Men long for a quick death but do not get it.

Five weeks to the Comoriscan islands. The inhabitants were well pleased and friendly, and sold Jón thirteen baskets of apples of many kinds. They were sweet and delicious, but after three nights were overripe and Jón had to throw them overboard, in tears, wishing they could drift back to Iceland.

A month of difficult sea, sailing past 11,000 islands and Arabian pirates; strict watches at night in a darkness one could almost hold, and all the constellations came back again upside-down. Ceylon. An empty castle, covered with moss, abandoned for hundreds of years. Exceedingly evil people had lived in it, and a heavy vengeance fell on them from the Lord; its name, Trinchlumala, meant "the abode of evil." None dared live there, except for two: Erik Grubbe, a Dane who failed on a mission to the Emperor and whose ship was lost, and a loyal servant. Because of his disgrace, Erik would not return home, and he lived hiding in the forest, hunting wild beasts. Jón and the men fired three shots to signal him, and left some linen clothes and victuals.

Two days to the Carmandel coast, and the Danish fort of Dansborg in the empire of Narsinga. As Dansborg had no harbor, the *Christianshavn* anchored far from land, near another Danish ship, the *Spaniel*. Flags raised, shots fired in salute all day, men shuttling from ship to ship exchanging news, wine, and carousal. Jón and a boatswain almost ended up in a duel over some gunpowder grime in the laundry tub; the two captains pulled out their rapiers when one made a joke about the other's wife's infidelity on his last voyage to the Indies. The men could not go ashore for two days because of a huge and terrible sea serpent, nine hundred ells long, until it was driven away by pouring castoreum, a bitter and fetid liquid made from the testicles of beavers, into the sea. A well-prepared captain has a secret store of a vial or two.

In 1620, a treaty had been concluded between the Danes and the King of Travanzour. Once a year a Danish ship would come with the wares the King most desired, silver and lead. In exchange, the King promised a full cargo of pepper, precious stones, gold and silver cloth, copper, graphite, silk and cotton, indigo dye, and other Indian goods. The King allotted a pleasant and smooth place by the sea where the Danes were to erect a fortress to be called Dansborg, 360 fathoms in circumference, with four watchtowers and a large tower; he assigned his master mason and five hundred men to complete the work. All Danish goods were first to be offered to the King. Indian natives were to be left in peace: if any Dane struck or killed an Indian, all Danes would be banished and their goods forfeited. No cattle could be slaughtered in the fort; no Dane could enter the Indians' pagodas, churches, or idol-houses, under punishment of death. The treaty was written and signed on golden paper.

New orders. Half the men of the *Christianshavn*, Jón among them, were to serve on shore in Dansborg, at a pay increase of one gulden, twenty fish, a month. To the sound of drums, pipes, and trumpets, Jón was mustered and reaffirmed his oath, swearing to be heedful in that foreign land. The *Spaniel* was to sail six weeks up the coast, to winter over in Ternasseri. The *Christianshavn* was to return to Denmark, and Jón wrote a letter to be carried to his brother Halldór, the first letter sent from the Indies to Iceland.

3.

Woolen cloth is not made here, for there is no wool.

It is so hot
it is as if one were standing next to a great fire,
the soles of the feet are always burning and
standing watch
one must keep turning like meat on a spit.

The palm trees are handsome,
planted in order like rows of soldiers.
They bear *carhanske* nuts, large as a child's head,
from which they make a butter as good as the best sour butter.
From that one tree, the palm tree,
they eat, drink, clothe themselves,
make fishing tackle and ships' cables and other gear,

build their ships and smacks of it,
and sew the seams together with its bark.

They hold cattle to be sacred, or to possess souls,
and therefore cows die natural deaths here.

The King himself worships a horned cow,
who lives in splendid rooms in the King's palace
with her own attendants,
and decorated with gold and precious stones and embroidery.
He visits her every morning and
washes his hands and face and even his mouth
in the cow's water.

They sit cross-legged on the floor and are very supple,
for they rub themselves with oil every day
and each other's bodies before going to sleep at night,
for the sake of their health,
and we have adopted their practice.

They have no strong drink,
but they chew a nut together with leaves and chalk
and spit out the juice.
Their mouths look bloody.

They make a wine out of palm tree juice
and sell it to the foreigners here:
Portuguese, Caffers, Praegiers, Selings, Moors,
Bengalians, Egyptians, Arabians, Moluchians, Javans,
English, Dutch, and Danish.

The King's throne
is made of marble and is as smooth as an egg.
As the King sits,
one man waves a fan above his head,
another holds a golden basin into which he spits his nut-juice.

The King had 900 concubines,
but he gave 300 of them to his son.

The concubines live in their own hall
with gilded pillars and windows of crystal glass, adorned
in gold and brocaded silk and pearls and jewels
and precious stones.
Once a year
they are permitted to walk outside, all together,
surrounded by the King's best fighting men.
When any die,
they are replaced by an equal number.
When the King dies,
they all must be burnt alive with him.

In every city there is one great temple,
called a *sinagoga* or *pagoga*,
built
of masonry with a high square tower
and a high stone wall all around.
Inside the wall
there is a large chariot
with shameful pictures too repulsive to describe.
There are idols of cows and goats and swine and buffaloes
(who resemble cattle but are not, and their milk is
like goat's milk).
On the rear wall of the temple
are their three chief gods,
called Suami, Rami, and Tameran.

Suami,
the chief of the gods,
has the countenance of a man and a trunk like an elephant,
with four talons and a crown on his head;
his face has an evil expression.
Rami
has no trunk but has talons and a crown.
Tameran looks like Rami.

There are harlots in the temple
who are hired out to the soldiers and the bachelors
every day for money,

and the money is put in the treasure-house of the temple.
The harlots dance
before the idols every night from nine to midnight,
and then the idols are carried out in the streets
with torches, fireworks, drum-beating, and dancing.
Goats are sacrificed to them with corn-sickles;
rice is offered to them
and red water is poured out.

There are many smaller temples
where lamps burn night and day.
There are groves with idols in them,
worshiped by the poor folk.

At night
they hold festivals, dances and strange games,
clothing themselves in various guises
with which they act out their idol-plays
with great skill by the light of fires and torches.
One of their plays
seemed to be like the story of Jonah
when the whale swallowed him.

They play a game where a man takes seven apples
in his left hand
and throws them up all around him with incredible speed
and as soon as they return to his hand
he throws them up again
so that they never stop
and circle round him like a wheel
and cannot be discerned individually
but are like a whirling line,
and in the end
they drop
one after the other
into his hand.

The sands of the beaches are as smooth as can be,
and when one walks in the eye of the sun,

one grain looks like beautiful gold
and the next like silver.

Their faith is such that they unashamedly worship Satan.
They believe that they must soothe him
with unceasing devotion and sacrifices
or he will unleash terrible evil upon them.

Three times a day
when someone dies,
the mourners stand outside the house
and beat themselves and bite their hands and flesh,
slap, scratch, pinch their faces,
fling themselves on the ground,
pour earth over their heads,
fill their mouths with it, shrieking with woe,
till they are bruised, bloody, and scarred.
The mourners are paid to do this, and the most violent
receive double.

They burn their corpses face down on a pile of dung.
Then they pick the bones out,
snow-white among the ashes,
and make a four-cornered pyramid out of them
for the ghost to live in.

These are some of their words:
sirka: woman   *avasari magni*: harlot   *abba*: oh father!
amma: oh mother!   *nica*: lord   *nerpa*: fire   *tanari*: water
tingra: to eat   *toccuna tingrani*: eat thou a little   *ni*: you
culcrani: drink ye   *culcrulidt*: jug   *pacra*: to look
ine pacrani: what are you looking for?   *angra*: to walk
ine angrana: where are you going?   *cumbride*: tall   *teyra*: milk
lette: curdled milk   *bumbarada*: musket   *spengardi*: small gun

Their laws are severe:
they have punishments for every crime.
They use hanging, breaking on the wheel, fire,
and many kinds of torture,

             bone-breaking, pinchings, starvation, and
                        serpent-bites.

                  A man and a woman
            were bolted together through their calves
                    with a large iron bolt
            and wandered naked about the palace.
                  No one knew their crime.

They sow their rice fields once a year and harvest it twice.
            There are no fields which produce meal.
        There is a sugar-tree which men suck and chew.
There is no honey, but many other kinds of fruits grow here.

            They make paper out of the palm tree leaves,
                     books out of the paper,
        and write with iron stiluses whatever they fancy,
    stories, ballads, poems, or whatever is their fashion.

        They make statuary and work well in copper,
                  in elephant bone and tusks,
            gold set with precious stones and pearls
        (which are found in seashells along the shore)
                     silver and brass.
                They are skillful in every kind
            of weaving and dyeing and painting cloth
                  with every kind of color,
        and the cloth is spread out in the sun to dry.
                     They have tinkers.

    Their shields are leather and stuffed with cotton,
    the soldiers use them for shelter from the midday sun.
                  They are skilled at arms,
        and have spears and swords with curved blades.

                  They marry off their children
                      as early as age four
                    and no later than ten.

The elephants
understand men's speech and have great understanding.
They lack only words.
They have no middle joint,
yet they lie down and take their rest.

Goods and labor are so cheap,
it is said the great temple was built
for only fifteen rixdollars in wages,
and nine fowls can be bought for six dried fish.

All the fishermen can swim like seals.
One day they caught a turtle,
larger than a skate, good and sweet eating.
Over its body grows a shell
hard as ivory and tough as horn.
It has four feet and claws on them all,
but when it lies still you see nothing of its feet.
It is so strong
it carried nine men from the church to the gate.
One small enough to put in your pocket
is strong enough to pull a single man.
How wondrous the works of God.

4.

In the fall of 1623, the *Christianshavn* returned home, ten months on the voyage, and the *Spaniel* sailed north to winter over. Of the men who remained in the fort, sixty died of the flux and about twenty survived to the spring.

The men were divided into messes of seven men each, sharing a single room where they slept and ate. Each mess was allotted an old Indian woman, who bore the water that had to be carried a long way, and an Indian boy to wash the linen. Watches served for three nights in a row, one man at each of the four corners of the fortress, standing in a little niche with a dome above it to keep out the rain that streamed down in the total darkness; napping while on watch was punishable by death. Jón's only other duty was to garble the pepper sent by the King of Travanzour, picking out the grass and stones with a large sieve. Sundays and Wednesdays there were sermons in the church.

A clerk named Morten got drunk and fell off the wall and died. Two soldiers, Stephen and Lars, got drunk and threatened the officers; they were put in irons and condemned to the swing-gallows. On the day of the execution, the other soldiers pleaded for leniency, and when the officers refused, the men raised their muskets at them with matches burning and the sentences were commuted.

A skillful carpenter named Cornelius, a gentle and courteous man, had fallen into misfortune back in Holland, and was under the evil influence of a sorceress whose granddaughter he had refused to marry. Temptations assailed him in his sleep and he would leap violently out of bed, disappear for a long time, and then return and lie weeping. One night the Englishwoman Temperance, wife of the clerk Hieronymus, saw him outside of the smithy having carnal intercourse with a goat. The next morning Cornelius went out the gate singing, dressed in his best suit, and was never seen again.

Nine men sailed north in a coasting vessel with lead for sale and were shipwrecked in a storm. They drifted to land, and came upon a great city of craftsmen and weavers called Meslapoten. The city was surrounded by the armies of the Mughal Sultan's son, Shah Jahan, who had been cruelly driven forth by his father, and who had taken the city with his soldiers and 11,000 elephants and 11,000 camels and 11,000 horses. Shah Jahan had a great liking for Christians, and gave the men his hospitality and gold coins and three suits of clothes, and issued letters of safe conduct home.

Jón fought and killed a huge poisonous serpent, striking such a blow that his sword was driven into the earth up to the hilt, a story he liked to tell at length. But he regretted not cutting out the tongue, for such are its medicinal powers that doctors will pay sixty rixdollars for it in Copenhagen and a hundred in Iceland.

A mile from town was a strange and curious sight which the men used to visit: a giant horse made of pasteboard and leather, with a rider upon it who had two faces, front and behind, with ferocious eyes. Nearby was a small temple where lamps of vegetable fat burned night and day. If no one was about, the men would sneak inside and extinguish the lamps, though Jón disliked that sport.

An Indian was possessed of an evil spirit, and an exorcist was sent for to drive out the devil by means of a shrill, resounding piece of copper which he struck with a hammer near the victim's ear. Jón watched the exorcist ask questions, and heard the unclean spirit reply: *Where had it come from?* From Trichlagour, where it had burnt down an entire street, and where it had found this man bathing in a pool. *How had this man offended the spirit?* By not offering it proper sacrifices. *How long would it possess the man?* Until the man offered two capons a year and certain measures of rice and tobacco and the *bita-larech* nut the Indians chew. The exorcist argued that the man was too poor to make such sacrifices, but finally an agreement was reached. As the unclean spirit departed, the man was seized with fits of yawning, trembling, spasms, foaming at the mouth, and then lay a long while as if dead. Then he leaped up, ran to a pool of water, jumped in, and staggered out in a daze. It was a long while before he became himself again.

The King of Travanzour sent envoys requesting six wag-onloads of lead, and the Rector of the fort refused. The King threatened to raze the fort to its foundations and sent his general, Calicut, with 40,000 soldiers, 1,100 horses, 1,100 camels, and 1,100 elephants to surround the fort. The men loaded their cannons with bar-shot, scissor-shot, chain-shot, and bunches of nine-inch nails bound with hempen thread, the points facing outward. Though the men in the fort were few, and sick and dying with the flux, the Lord put fear in Calicut's heart and he did not attack. After two weeks of siege, the

Spaniel returned from its wintering-over, and at the sight of it, Calicut retreated.

Jón went to visit two friends aboard the *Spaniel*, and was rejoiced by the sudden appearance of two ships sailing out of the south, with snow-white sails and flags flying from their mastheads: the huge *Pearl* and its smaller companion, the *Jupiter*. All the cannons and muskets were fired, the Indian merchants gathered on the shore, and the temple harlots danced.

The *Pearl* brought Admiral Rollant Crappe, famed voyager to the Indies, and General Calicut came to visit him, with nine palanquins, 500 fully accoutered servants, 500 soldiers in Turkish dress, nine elephants, and 500 horses. Lavish gifts were exchanged: among them, two well-polished bronze cannons for the King, with figures of people stamped upon them, which the King installed in his sleeping chambers; and for the Danish king, a bed of cedarwood, all inlaid with ivory. Hearing General Calicut's complaints, the Admiral reprimanded the Rector for endangering the lives of the men in the fortress and the goods of the King and the Danish East Indies Company. He commanded the Rector to sail on the long and dangerous journey to the Moluchas islands in quest of spices.

The Admiral's wrath fell too on the minister, Master Jens, who had secretly asked the barber to lance a sore on a privy part of his body. The barber went to the Admiral and told him that the sore had come from impure converse with the Indian women. Master Jens denied it, and the Admiral locked him in a solitary cell and forced him to take those medicines that reveal falsehood by making the hair and beard fall out. After nine days with no results, he too was ordered to sail on the *Jupiter* to the Moluchas, a voyage that only eight men survived, the Rector but not Master Jens among them.

Peace returned. Every Saturday, General Calicut sent three wild boars, so that the men in the fort would have fresh meat. And the King sent long trains of horses, elephants, camels, and oxen carrying pepper to load on the *Pearl*. The animals wore bells around their necks, and could be heard long before they were seen.

5.

Cargo worth ten tons of gold was stowed on the *Pearl*: three and a half lasts of pepper; cotton cloth, plain and patterned; silk and gold cloth; precious stones in five small bags; indigo dye; cotton half-woven with silk from the kingdom of Bengal which feels both silky and like fur to the touch; and other rare things seldom seen.

Those who wanted to return home could sail on the *Pearl*. Jón was reluctant, for its guns were old and in bad condition, but his friends persuaded him to sign on. A few days later, still in the harbor, firing a salute, Jón's cannon exploded and he was thrown overboard, and sank to the bottom of the sea, and was found floating face downward like an Indian corpse.

Three fingers on his right hand and half his left thumb were blown off; two other fingers on his left hand became useless; he was burned all over and had lost his hair and beard. The ship sailed on September 24, 1624; Jón lay in a sickbed his friends had constructed for fourteen weeks, and even after could perform few tasks.

With them on the journey was a parrot who could speak the Indian, Portuguese, and German tongues. After eleven weeks at sea, he fell ill, and bitterly upbraided the Captain for taking him on such a perilous voyage. He said that if he died it would be the Captain's fault, but if it were God's will he would consent. Three days later he died and was thrown overboard.

Hans the cook ran amuck with two large knives, threatening to kill the Captain. He was put in chains, freed after he begged forgiveness, then went after the Captain again with a red-hot fire-fork. The men began to fall sick of the dropsy and five

died. Jón bore a grudge against Master Arend, the surgeon's
mate, who had kept two of Jón's amputated fingers and laid
them in a special case, refusing to give them back, for sailors
believed that those who owned a dead finger would never
lose their way. Otherwise, till then, a voyage of routine and no
particular events.

Ninety miles from the Barbary Coast, on Palm Sunday itself,
after the sermon and dinner, the crew began an ugly sport
below deck, dancing and singing like the Indian temple harlots, and the game went too far. Jón grieved in spirit and
reproached them bitterly. That night he dreamt a dire dream.
Bartel the boatswain—a man who was quarreling with Jón—
came to him while he was sleeping, pulled off his bedclothes
and held a large knife at his throat, saying that he had been
commanded by God, the great King, to kill Jón and all the
ship's crew. Jón begged him to spare certain of his friends and
Bartel agreed, but the dream ended with Bartel outside the
cabin doors on the larboard side, crying, "You were playing
an evil sport, and now it is my turn."

The next day a contrary wind sprang up from the northeast;
the main-top sail was taken in, and the ship staggered under
the storm. The gale increased, and the maincourse and the
forecourse blew away like paper; in the great waves the ship
tossed like an empty box; the sails looked like strips of sea-
weed. The mainmast cracked and fell, crushing the two carpenters; the bow hit a wave and the bowsprit broke off the
stem head and the forestay gave out. The rigging was cut
away; the foremast broke loose from its stepping and was jet-
tisoned. All that was left was the mizzenmast. Men went to
the pumps, but although there were thirteen they could not
pump the ship clear.

Trumpets were blown for prayers and bells rung; the minister
exhorted them to repentance and contrition; they sang the
hymns "Hence I fare in peace" and "When sore our need."
The cable of the main anchor broke loose—300 fathoms long
and each fathom the weight of eighty dried cod—and flung

from side to side across the deck with each toss of the waves, breaking all the casks, barrels, and vessels, spilling all the wine, butter, meat, rice, peas and beans, and the tar and oil that mixed in with the food and spoiled it. Three terrible waves that seemed to fall from the sky struck in succession and carried away the rudder Jón had first seen when it was freshly cut with no iron on it. The Captain lay weeping in his berth.

When the storm passed they were far out in the Western Main; 150 sea-miles to Spain and 500 to England; without rudder, provisions, or sails; the men weak with dropsy; the few remaining bits of bread were found to be covered with cockroaches. Some argued for killing the ship's cat to eat. A tiny vessel of Biscayans appeared and sailed around them twice, but thinking the ship had been in a battle did not dare to come aboard, and despite the crew's entreaties sailed on.

The ship drifted toward England in fair weather, then a storm from the southeast drove them almost to the coast of Iceland, where it would have been too dangerous to land without rudder or proper sail. Fog and foul weather; eight weeks at sea; the dropsy causing the men to swell like bladders filled with air; fifteen died. A sight of the Scilly Isles and the men rejoiced, but a storm blew them back to sea; only three men strong enough to steer the ship with makeshift sails; the rest sprawled or crawling on their knees. Then land: Ireland: a village called Youghal, where men in herring-busses sailed out to rescue the ship.

Two died on the crossing to land; two died at the first taste of fresh food; the Captain died. The men were given beef, lamb, strong beer, biscuits, rye bread, butter, French brandy, Spanish wine, French communion wine, two kinds of salt, vinegar, herbs, distilled spirits, and tobacco. Jón was asked whether he wanted food or drink. He chose drink, and after pots of ale, tied a rope around each wrist to prop himself up, and lost consciousness for a day. Four more died. June 4, 1625: of the 143 who sailed out on the *Pearl* in September, 75 were left.

The Irish people took the men in and showed them great hospitality. The land was good, fertile, and fair, and Jón had never seen such fat sheep. Two gentlemen passengers were sent to Denmark to advise the King and the Company of their situation and to arrange for repairs. They were delayed a month in London, where thousands were dying every day of the plague. When they reached Copenhagen, they found the King had gone to Germany to fight the Emperor and the Papists in the war that would last thirty years and see the pillage of many Danish towns.

The men waited over a year in Ireland. Hans, the same cook who had run amuck on board the ship, ran a sword through the Rector's chest and was hanged on the gallows. When help finally came, it was decided that those who were too weak or disabled to assist in the repairs should travel by land and sea to Copenhagen. Jón left the goods he had brought from India—worth 600 rixdollars there and 6,000 in Europe—on the *Pearl*, to be carried to Denmark when the ship was seaworthy.

Jón could no longer make his living from his hands, and his goods had not arrived. He applied to the Company under the terms of his contract, which awarded compensation for injuries suffered on the job. But the contract granted different sums for the loss of a right or left hand, and Jón had lost three fingers on the right, and half the thumb and the use of two fingers on the left, but not the entirety of either hand, so the Company decided that the matter needed more consideration, and delayed paying. Nor could he appeal to the King, who was away in Germany and taken up with the invasion of his lands.

Jón longed to go back to Iceland after eleven years, and arranged to sail with some merchants, giving an honest man, Søren the tailor, power of attorney to collect his goods and compensation. The *Pearl* returned to Copenhagen the day after he left, but the Company would not hand over Jón's goods.

At his age thirty-three, Jón, Ólaf's son, now known as the
India-traveler, had become a man of mark and a welcome
guest in the houses of persons of high station, where he would
pass the winters telling the stories of his voyages. He married
Ingibjörg, Ólaf's daughter, the twin sister of Randíður, his
brother Halldór's wife. They lived in Áltafjörður with Jón's
kinsfolk. It was said that Ingibjörg had quarreled with a
woman who had put a curse on her, and she drowned when a
small boat in which she was traveling to visit friends capsized.
Jón married Þorbjörg, Einar's daughter, and, as it had been
foretold by the mysterious man named Frederick, they had a
son, Ólaf. Jón oversaw a small farm, and wrote many letters to
the King and to the Company, asking for his compensation
and his goods, with no result. Þorbjörg died in old age, and
Jón mourned her for two years. Ólaf, Jón's son, wrote in the
parish ledger that his father, Jón, Ólaf's son, the India-traveler, called on his Savior and fell sweetly asleep in the Lord on
the Eve of the Inventio Crucis, May 2, 1679, in his eighty-sixth
year.

[1998]

II

IN THE ZÓCALO

Nietzsche, dying, dreamed of moving to Oaxaca to recover his health. Others, myself among them, have dreamed of dying and then moving to Oaxaca. For at any moment, if for only a moment, where I want to be is in its zócalo.

It is more than the travel-magazine comfort of sitting for hours on the raised platform of the café, looking out over the cobblestone streets without cars, the orange blossoms in the canopy of the flame trees, the balloon vendors dwarfed in a kitsch explosion of pink and silver mylar, the kids playing good-natured hide-and-seek with the local halfwit, the strange silence that presses down on the square, even when thousands are viewing the whimsically carved vegetable tableaux on the Night of the Radishes. And it is more than the sensation of being enveloped in the salubrious climate Nietzsche dreamed of—a weather that, in the north, we receive for one or two days in late spring, and remember. The Oaxaca zócalo is more than the most beautiful Plaza Mayor in Mexico. More than the others, it fulfills the function of all zócalos: a place for doing nothing, sitting at the center of the universe.

A city, traditionally, does not merely contain a sacred or secular center. It *is* a center, surrounded by streets and houses, and from that still center, the "unwobbling pivot" of Confucianism, the power of the city emanates; around it the comings and goings of the world turn. Han Ch'ang-an, two thousand years ago, was the most literal manifestation of this: laid out in the form of the Big and Little Dippers, with the Emperor's Glittering Palace at the place of the unmoving North Star.

In times of insecurity, as in medieval Europe, the center is found amidst a maze of winding, easily defended streets, all within the confines of defensive moats and walls. In moments of imperial confidence, the city is arranged in a grid, emblem of the new order that has overcome the previous chaos.

Mohenjo-daro was the first of the many grid cities, and later, after the luminous Dark Ages, the Italian Renaissance rediscovered the grid, inspired—it is very Italian—by the chessboard: the little orderly squares as the stage for intrigues, strategies, and assassinations. The Spanish took it from the Italians, and within four years of Columbus' first voyage were erecting their first grid city, Santo Domingo, on the island of Hispaniola. By 1580, there were 273 similar cities throughout New Spain.

[Conquest followed by the replication of monuments to one's self: it is the norm in the West, from the arches of the Romans to the arches of McDonald's. In contrast, consider this bit of Chinese intelligence: when the legendary Founding Emperor Shih Huang-ti defeated a city, he had an exact replica of its palace built in his own capital, to house and retain the vital forces that had once given strength to the fallen city. The Romans, in so many things a conjunction of East and West, gave a proto-capitalist twist to this Asian practice: the *evocatio*, in which the local deities of besieged cities were invoked and persuaded to move to Rome, where they would enjoy greater powers.]

Few of the Spanish colonial cities—the great exceptions being México-Tenochtitlán and Cuzco—were built over the pre-Columbian cities: a New World must have its new world order. Oaxaca itself wandered and changed names for a few years: first in 1520 as Villa de Segura de la Frontera near the Zapotec town of Tepeaca; then to the Aztec fort of Huaxyácac; then south to the coast, to the Mixtec kingdom of Tututepec, where the climate was too tropical and the natives hostile; and then back again in 1522 to Huaxyácac, as the town of Antequera, and later—it is unclear when—as Oaxaca, the original Náhuatl name having been transformed by Spanish mumbling.

In 1529, the great urban planner of the Empire, Alonso García Bravo, architect of Mexico City and Veracruz, was sent to erect a grid over the razed buildings of the small Aztec fort. The zócalo he laid out—precisely aligned, as centers always are, to the cardinal points—was exactly 100 by 100 *varas* square. To the north, the Aztec direction of death, was to be the cathedral. To the south, municipal buildings. No walls were needed to keep the barbarians out: from the zócalo this

balance of sacred and secular power would radiate unob-
structed throughout the valley.

   To sit in the silence of the zócalo in Oaxaca—a silence that
is not from the absence of motion, but rather as though sound
had been erased, vacuumed out, from human activity—is to
recover that state of perfect rest that can only occur at the center, and that is now so noticeably absent from most of our
cities and most of our lives. To dream of sitting in the zócalo
in Oaxaca is not to imagine an escape from the world, a ship-
wreck on a tropical island, but rather an existence—one that
can only last a few moments—at the heart of the world: to be
completely in the world, but without distraction.

   And yet, as always in Mexico, order is subverted, sym-
metry set askew. The central axis at Teotihuacán does not pass
through the Temple of Quetzalcóatl; Monte Albán, Mitla,
Chichén Itzá, and so many other sites are similarly slightly,
intentionally dislocated. Is it an image of the imperfection of
the human world that can imitate, but never rival, heaven? Or
is it the emblem of becoming, of forms that are almost, but
never quite, fixed? Time, in pre-Columbian Mexico, might
have been a nest of perfect circles, one within the other, but
the dominant forms of its arts were the spiral and the jagged
steps. Spiral: from a central point of origin whirling into the
unknown. Jagged steps: an indirect way to get from one point
to another, a way of stages and rests.

   In the zócalo in Oaxaca, one is planted at the center and
pulled in two directions. Physically, to the north, to the adjoin-
ing little raised plaza beside and the Alameda in front of the
cathedral, another hubbub of activity, and a reminder that,
slightly off-center, there is always another center. And
metaphorically, or historically, to the south, a block from the
zócalo, where the municipal market now stands, and where
there is the ghost of another center, that of the razed town of
Huaxyácac. In its day it too was an ordered and quartered
city: six hundred men with their wives and children from each
of the principal Aztec provinces, each in their own quarter:
Mexicanos, Texcocanos, Tepanecas, Xochimilcas, with other
groups scattered on the outskirts.

There are two things to do in the zócalo. First, one must circumambulate, as the new kings of China or Egypt or Cambodia, upon their coronations, were required to circle the sacred center. Circumambulation stakes out one's place in the world; in its democratic form, a territory to inhabit, not to own or rule. Second, one must sit in that place and let the world continue on. It is an act that is natural in Mexico—as sacred and natural as washing one's hands in India. Yet it is unimaginable in certain other cultures: here, for example, one needs to join an alternative religious group to sit without embarrassment.

Sitting in the zócalo, one's eyes are invariably drawn to the center of the center, to the ornate and Ruritanian bandshell. It is the great late European contribution to this concept of sacred space: that at the absolute center is not a cosmic tree or sacred mountain or pillar of stone—ladders between heaven and earth—but rather an enclosure of empty space. The word *bandshell* captures it perfectly: *band*, the source of music; *shell*, a bounded hollow, a seashell you hold to your ear.

In Oaxaca, the high raised platform of the bandshell is forbidden space, inaccessible to the public—though the children, as if in an ancient parable, always manage to find a way in. Empty by day, crowded with local musicians at night. Who cares if the music is less than ethereal? The image that one dreams of is this: at the center of the universe is a perfect and perfectly aligned square; at its center is an empty space; and, at the end of the day, that space is filled with music, a music to reenact the sound that created the universe, the sound that will invent the following day. Time turns, the world turns, around that pivot. Where I want to be is there.

[1993]

NAKED MOLE-RATS

Naked mole-rats have no fur, but their lips are hairy. Their pinkish mottled skin is loose and hangs in folds, like something that has lost a great deal of weight, the easier to squirm through their narrow tunnels. Incisors protrude from their mouths like pincers, the only feature of their undefined faces. One naked mole-rat can fit across your fingers, its tail dangling down. They have been under the earth for at least three million years.

They never surface. They are blind. Their world is not a labyrinth, but a straight tunnel, a mile or two long, with innumerable cul-de-sacs branching off, and certain larger chambers. They live on the tuberous roots that grow towards them.

As many as three hundred inhabit a colony, moving a ton of dirt every month. They have a caste system, tripartite like the Indian. The smallest among them are the diggers and food-gatherers who work through the night in a line, male and female equally, the first gnawing the earth and kicking it back to the next, who kicks it back, until the last, who digs a temporary hole to the surface, kicks out the dirt, its rump exposed to the moon and predators, and then plugs the hole again. When they come across a root, they chew off pieces to carry to the others.

The medium-sized are the warriors, who try to fend off the rufous-beaked snakes, the file snakes, the white-lipped snakes, and the sand boas that sometimes find their way in. They attack with repeated tiny bites that are, if the snake is small enough, mysteriously instantly fatal. When, by chance, two colonies of naked mole-rats tunnel into each other, their warriors fight to the death.

These castes serve the largest, who are the breeders. Unique among mammals, only one female reproduces. She is by far the longest and the fattest and the most aggressive in the colony. If she dies there is chaos. She is attended by one to three males, who do nothing else. They spend their time nuzzling her; have sex, initiated by her, by mounting her from behind for fifteen seconds, bracing themselves by holding their front legs against the walls of the tunnel, and mainly failing. When she becomes pregnant, the teats of every colony member, male and female, enlarge, reach their peak at the birth, and then shrink. Just before birth, the female runs wildly through the tunnels.

She has four or five litters a year of a dozen pups. The babies have transparent skin through which their internal organs are clearly visible. Only a few survive, and they live long lives, twenty years or more. The dead babies are eaten, except for their heads. At times the live ones are eaten too.

Interbred so long, they are virtually clones. One dead-end branch of the tunnel is their toilet: they wallow there in the soaked earth so that all will smell alike. They are nearly always touching each other, rubbing noses, pawing, nuzzling. When their tunnel is blocked they work from both sides and reconnect it perfectly. They sleep in a packed heap in the nesting chamber, with the breeders on the top, staying warm, each naked mole-rat with its nose pressed against the anus and genitals of another.

They are continually cruel in small ways, clanking teeth, breathing rapidly into each other's open mouths, batting, swiping, biting, pulling one another's baggy skin, shoving each other sometimes a yard down the tunnel. But only the females who compete for the role of breeder inflict real harm. Wounded, the defeated female crouches shivering in the toilet, ignored by the others until she dies.

The tunnels are never silent. Naked mole-rats make at least seventeen sounds: soft chirps and loud chirps, high-pitched and low, tooth-grinding, trills, twitters, tongue-taps, sneezes, screams, hisses, grunts. Different sounds for when they bump into each other, when they piss, when they mate, when they're disturbed, alarmed, wounded, when they shove each other, when they meet a foreigner such as a beetle, when they find food, when they can't find food.

They clean their feet with their teeth. They clean their teeth with their feet. They yawn. They shiver. They scratch themselves after they piss. They bask near the surface, in the warm sunless earth. They doze with their short legs splayed, their huge heads drooping. They double over, mouth to anus, to eat their own shit.

They scurry with eyes closed, forward or backward at the same speed, over and under each other. They change direction by somersaulting. They find their way, when they don't know it, by darting forward till their nose bumps the wall, dart backward, adjust the angle, dart forward again. Sometimes a naked mole-rat will suddenly stop, stand on its hind-legs, and remain motionless, its head pressed against the roof of the tunnel. Above its head is the civil war in Somalia. Their hearing is acute.

[1995]

GENUINE FAKES

About ten years after it was published, an energetic young man retyped Jerzy Kosinski's 1965 prize-winning novel, *The Painted Bird*, gave the manuscript a new title, and submitted it to a dozen American publishers. None of them, including Kosinski's own publisher, recognized the book, and all of them rejected it.

It was a good joke, and a telling comment on how books get published, but the story does not end there. Some years before Kosinski's death, an investigative journalist wrote an article claiming that the Polish-born author could not possibly have written *The Painted Bird* in English: at the time, he was a recent immigrant to the United States, and his command of the language was poor. It was suggested that he either wrote the novel in Polish and had it translated, or he outlined the story to an assistant who actually "wrote" the book. Either way, the book's acclaimed verbal pyrotechnics would not be the work of Kosinski. Furthermore, there were rumors that the novel was based on—or possibly plagiarized from—the writings of an unpublished Polish writer who had died in a concentration camp, and whose manuscript had somehow fallen into Kosinski's possession.

The Painted Bird is a classic case of how authorship determines reception. The memoir of a small boy in war-torn Poland, it would have been enveloped in an almost unbearable pathos if it had been the work of the murdered Pole. As it is, although the text remains the same, its importance diminishes according to the identity of its author, in the following order: Kosinski as original writer, the translator, the assistant, Kosinski as plagiarist, the young re-typist. As Salvador Dali said, the first person to compare a woman's cheeks to a rose was undoubtedly a genius; the second person to do so could easily have been an idiot.

Forgery is the little pin that pricks the hot-air balloon of theories of art. Intellectually, we may believe, with the modernists, that in art all ages are contemporaneous—that a lyric

by Sappho has the immediacy of a poem written yesterday—
or believe, with the so-called postmodernists, that there is no
author, only the text. But the actual reading or looking or lis-
tening to a work of art always occurs in the tension between
our perception of the work itself and our knowledge of its origin. Even when the author is Anonymous (as the old joke
goes, the greatest writer who ever lived) the work is inextricably placed in its historic moment. Its timelessness is its
unchanging core, which keeps the work alive over the centuries. But its location in time—moreover in a time that is
receding—also keeps the work in constant flux. We see the
work as part of an archaic context, a context we must enter
into, but we see it with modern eyes—that is, with the eyes of
a modernity that is always changing.

A forgery is an object without a creator, and human nature
cannot bear anything without a narrative of its origin. (The
liveliest debate in physics today is the question that every age
and culture has had to answer: what happened in the first seconds of the universe?) There is no reason why an exact copy
(assuming it were possible) of a painting should be inferior to
the original, but we *know*, emotionally if not rationally, that it
is so. Mark Twain said that Wagner's music was better than it
sounds. A forgery is always worse than it looks.

Forgery is based on authenticity, and both of them are
jokes. But it is authenticity, not forgery, that is the cruelest joke
of all. The Metropolitan Museum buys a Greek vase for a million dollars that is hailed as the masterpiece of its kind, until
it is revealed as a fake. We venerate Da Vinci's *Last Supper*,
even though it has been restored so many times it no longer
has any of its original paint. We ponder the quite serious critical proposal that the plays of Shakespeare were not written
by William Shakespeare, but by another man of the same
name. Yesterday's attribution to the hand of the Master
becomes today's relegation to an anonymous "From the stu-
dio of . . ." Nothing is more certain than the foolishness of old
certainties.

But if authenticity leaves a taste of bitter regret, forgery at
its best is a bit of hilarity. When it is done for monetary gain it
is as humorless as a counterfeit bill: all skill and no wit. When

it is a work of megalomania it is at its most perverse, the combination of skill and obsession that leads to the pleasure of
seeing one's efforts hanging in a museum or sold at Sotheby's.
But the perversity of the humor is that it can never be shared:
the forger must laugh alone. Forgery is at its most comic when
it is an act of simple revenge, and when that act is, in the end,
revealed.

For example, the pianist Alexis Weissenberg was tired of
reading reviews that claimed he was a "cold, unemotional"
performer. So he invented—what else?—a soundless piano.
He then gave a concert where he played a tape recording of
himself, and accompanied the music with precisely coordinated histrionic gestures and passionate grimaces. The critics
naturally hailed the evening as one of Weissenberg's most
moving performances, and the pianist triumphantly revealed
the hoax.

An elaborate combination of revenge and megalomania,
and one with more serious consequences, was the case of the
century's greatest (known) forger, Hans van Meegeren. Born
in Holland in 1889, he had some success as a very young
artist, most notably for a drawing of Queen Juliana's pet deer,
which still appears on Dutch Christmas cards. But the dread-
ful Symbolist canvases he began painting in his late twenties
were receiving the kind of reviews usually reserved for misunderstood genius or well-understood mediocrity. Needing
money, he made his first forays into the forging business by
producing fakes of Hals, Ter Borch, and de Hoogh. They sold
moderately well. He then discovered his true mission in life,
the master plan:

Vermeer had recently been rediscovered, and was rightly
being celebrated as a rival to Rembrandt as the avatar of
Dutch genius. There was, however, a large chronological gap
in Vermeer's thirty-odd known works: his early years when,
it was thought, he had traveled to Italy, fallen under the influence of Caravaggio, and painted works with religious
themes—unlike his later landscapes, interiors, and portraits.
As it happened, the art critics who were indulged in speculat-
ing on Vermeer's missing paintings were the very same who
had consigned van Meegeren to the Siberia of taste.

It was perfect. Van Meegeren went into seclusion in France and, after years of perfecting the preparation of materials that would delude scientific examination—to this day some of his techniques cannot be explained—he proceeded to produce the missing Vermeers. His greatest work, *The Supper at Emmaus*, was declared by one critic—a particular enemy of van Meegeren's own paintings—to be not only authentic, but "*the* masterpiece of Vermeer." The painting was sold in 1937 for the equivalent of $1.4 million, and it hung, to great adulation, in the Boysman Museum for seven years.

It would, perhaps, still be there were it not for the inevitable twist of fate. After the Second World War, it was discovered that van Meegeren had sold a Vermeer to Hermann Göring. He was arrested for stealing a Dutch National Treasure and selling it to the enemy. To escape a conviction of treason, van Meegeren was forced to confess that the painting was a fake—and moreover, that all the newlyfound Vermeers were van Meegerens. He was not believed, and the police insisted he produce a Vermeer in prison, which he did. Yet despite his confession and conviction for forgery—he died in prison soon after—there were some critics who stubbornly maintained that *The Supper of Emmaus* was indeed a genuine Vermeer that the forger was claiming as his own. They successfully pleaded with the Dutch government not to destroy the painting, in case a mistake had been made. (The argument, curiously, against capital punishment.) Finally, in an odd reversal, the pop novelist Irving Wallace published an article in 1947 celebrating van Meegeren as a hero who had swindled Göring. (We now know that van Meegeren was a Nazi sympathizer who had no choice when Göring asked for the painting.)

Looking at *The Supper of Emmaus* today, it seems incredible that this unspeakably clumsy canvas was ever mistaken for the real thing. As an authentic Vermeer, it is pathetic. But as an original van Meegeren it is a brilliant parody which, in one startling gesture, both delivers the last laugh and anticipates postmodern ironic/iconic pastiche: van Meegeren clearly copied the face of Jesus from a photograph of Greta Garbo.

Forge: the same word for falsifying artworks and shaping metal by heating and hammering. In traditional societies, the blacksmith, the maker of the weapons, is, like the shaman, a source of great power who is kept apart from the rest of the community through a web of taboos. In our society, it is the forger who has taken the Romantic ideals of the isolation of the artist to its greatest extreme. He is a maker of art who can never be acknowledged as such, whose work is acclaimed while he remains in total anonymity. He is an outcast from the outcasts of society. And yet, he is also the purest artist: the one who rejects the cult of personality, who has no identity and no personal style, who believes only in the work itself and the age to which it is attributed. The forger, in the end, may be the model artist.

[1995]

SEX OBJECTS

Zebra finches like their males with red legs and females with
black legs, and are repelled by males with green legs or
females with blue legs. A female Australian brush turkey is
attracted to the male who builds her the largest nest, and is
quite demanding: the nests can run to two tons. An Archbold
bowerbird is especially smitten by a male capable of procur-
ing rare King of Saxony bird of paradise blue feathers to feath-
er the bower. A female tern prefers the male who presents her
with the most fish; an emphid fly takes the one who produces
the prettiest hollow silk balloons.

Guppies like their guppies bright orange; pupfish like
their pupfish blue; squid like a squid whose skin changes
color. A cichlid looks at the inside of the throat, a fiddler crab
at the single giant claw, turned blue, waving from the beach.
A grackle wants a male who can sing more than one song. A
female sage grouse will always take the best dancer, even if he
has already mated with thirty others that day. A roach fish
counts the number of bumps on a male's body. Female pea-
cocks, as everyone knows, go for flashy tails. Swallows and
widow birds and malachite sunbirds like their male tails long;
great snipes want the whitest. Red jungle fowls look at the
eyes and the comb, and couldn't care less about feathers. A
cockroach watches the male do push-ups.

An aphid looks out for wings; the asexual variety don't
have any. A male black grouse will mate with anything that
looks vaguely like a female black grouse, even a wooden
model. An Indian moon moth can smell a female miles away.
Male hairless chimpanzees go for the pinkest and most
swollen rear end. Bonobos—pygmy chimps—just have sex
all the time. A female tortoise loves any male that butts her on

the head; a rabbit any male who pees on her and shows his fluffy tail.

Sappho comes down to us only in the bits of papyrus used to wrap mummies, but some of the lineaments of her desire have survived. She wants—paraphrasing the Davenport translation—a woman slender as a young tree, with thin hands, and wrists like the wild rose. Eyes that are bold, or with a smiling brightness, beautiful feet, and something that has been lost in the lacunae, skin presumably, whiter than milk, whiter by far than an egg.

She loves violet breasts, and violet softness, the way the long pleats of a dress move, hair tied with red yarn, and a crown of flowers and dill on curly hair. The voice must be more melodious than a harp, more harmonious than lyres; a pleasing voice, with honey in its words. And an odor—though exactly which is now unknown. She is attracted to a country girl too ignorant to arrange her dress, or women wrapped in rich shaggy wool, with purple handkerchiefs, red dresses, robes the color of peaches, with Asian deerhide shoes, or Asian leather shoes with Lydian patterns across the toes. A girl picking a flower just opened, softer than a fine dress, tenderer than a rose, graceful, decorous, suave, more golden than gold, like an apple, like a mountain hyacinth.

Sappho's mating grounds are a grove of apple trees, where horses munch on wildflowers, or on the cushions of soft beds. Her courtship rituals include drinking nectar in golden cups, plaiting garlands of roses and violets in one another's hair, leather phalluses, and aromatic oils. She falls asleep against the breast of a friend, [lacuna] slick with slime. Her desire is like wind in the mountain forests. Jealousy makes her tongue stick to her dry mouth, and a thin fire spread beneath her skin.

Haddock knock, crabs rasp, mosquitoes coo, swiftlets click, racket-tailed hummingbirds make a racket with their tails, male spiders pluck a rhythm on the female's web. A female canary must hear the song of her mate for her ovaries to develop; the more he sings, the faster this goes. The male echidna drugs the female with a mild poison from a spur on his heel. Crocodiles and minks simply rape.

Fungi have tens of thousands of sexes; earthworms are hermaphrodites; slime molds have thirteen genders, all of which mate with each other in different ways. A slipper limpet floats on the sea as a male, then turns into a female when it attaches itself to a rock. Bdelloid rotifers are all female; they refresh their gene pool by eating their dead sisters. In the mating season, all the males of the Australian marsupial mouse die from the strain.

Sappho's most vivid fragment, one that needs no other lines above or below it, reads, in Davenport's translation, in its entirety:

"You make me hot."

[1996]

THE STORY OF OM

In the 1960's, people read "magical realist" novels and repeated rumors that were as fantastic as the fiction. In the 1970's, the investigative journalists revealed that the realities of the previous decade had been even more implausible. No underground newspaper could have invented stories as magically realist as the CIA's quite serious plots to send Fidel Castro a box of exploding cigars, or to place a powder in his shoes that would make his beard fall out.

One of my favorite anecdotes in the 1960's was, thanks to its cheesy stereotypings, the most difficult to believe: A friend of a friend is staying in an apartment in the East Village. One muggy August night, he hears some celestial music coming from somewhere outside, looks out the window, and sees on the fire escape a few floors above him a beautiful young woman playing "A Love Supreme" on the saxophone. She is completely naked.

He climbs the fire escape to talk to her. She tells him that she and her friends are devotees of Om. She gestures toward the apartment window. Inside are eight or ten equally beautiful young women, lounging about, largely undressed.

Suddenly the door opens, and an enormous black man—seven feet tall and wide as a wrestler—walks in. The women leap to their feet, crying "Om! Om!" and drape themselves over him. Om sees my friend's friend on the fire escape and glares at him, saying nothing. The man scurries off, never daring to return. But every night, for the week he is staying in the apartment, he hears the crashing sounds of John Coltrane's "Om" played over and over on the stereo all night long.

I had forgotten the story until, a few weeks ago, Om unexpectedly appeared. I happened to be reading a long article in a Mexican newspaper about bizarre nightlife in L.A. Somewhere in the middle, for no apparent reason, a paragraph flashed back to a scene in Mexico City, years before: The author and her sister are in an apartment with a dozen beautiful young women, naked under transparent baby doll dresses, who worship an enormous black man named Om.

I called the writer, whom I knew. She told me that a paragraph from another piece she was writing for the same newspaper had inexplicably been inserted into her article, and yes, she had indeed met Om. In 1978—ten years after my story—she and her sister were approached on a street in Mexico City by two young American women who asked them if they could translate something from English into Spanish. The four of them went to a dingy apartment, inhabited by these underdressed Americans, each with a child of approximately the same age. The women said that they belonged to a new religion that worshiped a goddess whose prophet was named Om, and they wanted the Mexicans to translate some of their sacred hymns and poetry.

Suddenly the door opened—my story, which I hadn't mentioned, was repeating itself—and in walked "the largest man I've ever seen in my life—he could barely fit through the door frame." Om offered the Mexicans wine, but soon became "aggressively flirtatious," and they left. For weeks after, the women kept calling, but the writer and her sister, though fascinated, were too frightened to go back.

The journalist's story continued: About five years later, a fourteen-year-old girl with drug problems, whom she knew, was picked up on the street by a couple of the Om women and taken back to their apartment. There, the girl, a virgin, was ritualistically deflowered by Om on a table in front of the other women and their children. She joined the group, which moved on to Oaxaca, and was finally kidnapped back by her parents. Around 1985, the journalist told me, Om was arrested for check fraud and deported from the country. There have been no further sightings.

Om, where are the cults of yesteryear? The group that used to set up long tables in Washington Square Park with huge glass jars of human brains in formaldehyde, damaged and deranged, they said, by white sugar. The teenagers who would demonstrate rug shampooers on a corner of Eighth Street, where the pedestrians were more likely to have carpets,

if at all, more cigarette-scarred than soap-sudsed. They were
runaways who lived in squalor in a Times Square apartment,
disciples of a former vacuum cleaner salesman who had
decoded the Bible, and rug shampooing was their spiritual
discipline. The American branch of Aum Shinrikyo—the ones
who released nerve gas in the Tokyo subway—whose head-
quarters was once at 53 Crosby Street in Soho, and who published an "Enlgish Version" of the Supreme Initiation teachings of their leader, Master Shoko Asahara: "Even if such a
global war as to be called World War 3 breaks out in 1999,
2001, or 2003, it is not a big problem for one who has attained
emancipation by that time. 'Something flashed (flash of
nuclear bombs). Okay I will enter Clear-light.' In this way you
can throw away your physical body."

And where is Mel Lyman, who vanished in 1975? A banjo
player in the once popular Jim Kweskin Jug Band, Lyman
founded the Boston underground paper *Avatar*, claimed he
was the reincarnation of Lincoln and Emerson (whose lives
overlapped, but no matter), was photographed by Diane
Arbus, and wrote a book called *The Autobiography of a Savior*,
calling himself Melvin Christ, or sometimes simply God. He
formed a "family" around him in the 1960's that lived off the
estate of the painter Thomas Hart Benton, whose daughter
was a stalwart. In 1973, three of them robbed a Boston bank,
supposedly at Lyman's command, supposedly as a protest
against Watergate. One was shot dead; another, Mark
Frechette—the star of Antonioni's *Zabriskie Point*—died mysteriously in prison.

At last report—some magazine articles in the 1980's—the
Lymans, as they called themselves, were based in the former
Eastman (Kodak) mansion in Hollywood, with twenty other
estates around the country, rich from a multimillion-dollar
construction business that remodeled the homes of movie
stars. With framed photos of Mel in every room and his gold
fork in a wooden box in the dining room, they addressed one
another by first name plus the person's astrological sign, had
a tape recorder running continually, and gathered nightly to
watch and discuss *Gunsmoke*, Mel's favorite show, or old
movies from "The Lord's List." When a Lyman male wanted

coffee, he raised his cup an inch off the table, and a Lyman female instantly filled it.

I think of Mel Lyman often—and not when drinking coffee—because of something I remember, perhaps incorrectly, that Jim Kweskin said in an interview, decades ago: After months of living together, Kweskin realized that Mel Lyman was truly God, because every time Mel made a phone call, the line was never busy, and the person he was calling was always home.

[1996]

POLITICAL ANALYSTS IN
MEDIEVAL INDIA

In medieval India, one of the best sources for reliable political commentary, as well as informed speculation on the future, was a dog. The practice was widespread for centuries, but the most detailed surviving description of it comes from an encyclopedia compiled in 1363 by a certain Shārngadhara, a Brahmin functionary in the desert kingdom of Mewar, now part of Rajasthan, and recently translated in part by the Indologist David Gordon White. Shārngadhara advises us that "in answer to the question *What is happening in the world?*, a mortal may place his entire trust" in five creatures: the fawn, the spotted owl, the crow, the female jackal, and the dog. Like any other roundtable of commentators, however, not all of these were equally persuasive. In fact, "The first four are, by their nature, barely intelligible. The dog is far easier to understand."

Of course, not merely any dog could become a political analyst. It had to be young, healthy, without defects and, above all, entirely black, presumably to insure that its opinions were consistent and unwavering, not mottled with qualifications or doubt. Working as it did in a royalist milieu, its tail, naturally, could not "bend to the left."

In appreciation from its grateful public, the opining dog was ritually bathed at sundown, and given a feast of milk and special cakes made in the shape of dogs: a practice that was refreshingly candid about the dog-eat-dog nature of politics. It was then placed in its forum, a multicolored mandala painted on the ground, and—this being India—was honored at exceeding length with songs, prayers, incense, lamps, flowers, food, and ritual fires. At dawn, having undoubtedly dozed through such welcoming remarks, the dog was ready to impart its expertise.

Generally speaking, things were going quite well in the kingdom if the dog scratched its head with its right forepaw, scratched its left paw with its right paw, scratched its right ear with its right paw, urinated with its right hind leg raised or, if female, scratched its belly. There were grave problems with the government if the dog yawned, vomited, ran away, hiccupped, coughed, seemed anxious, fell asleep and shook violently, dug a hole, howled, or looked into the sun.

As a kingdom's fate is largely dependent on the members of its royal family, the dog was especially valued for its insights into the inner palace. Its bark could indicate whether any acts committed by the king in a previous life would have consequences in the present day. The manner in which it urinated was a discussion of dynastic continuity: whether the pregnant queen would give birth to a son or daughter, or miscarry. If the dog lay down without scratching itself, someone in the royal household was gravely ill. The dog also knew who would live to old age, who would soon die, what important emissaries were on the way, whether the queen had a lover, and even whether the lover was someone within the palace or an outsider. In perhaps its most arcane form of commentary, a female dog could reveal that the king's enemies were plotting against him at that very moment by attempting to have sex—Shārngadhara does not explain how—with a young bull at a crossroads.

Like many strident editorialists, the dog tended to urge courses of action which would not directly affect it. For example: "A dog may encourage a king to go into battle." This was not, however, uninformed jingoism. The dog was equally an expert on military strength: "When two armies are locked in battle, it can tell which will win the undisputed victory, which will deal the crushing blow." Canine analysis was particularly useful in times of hostility between two kingdoms: If the dog faced east, there would be war. If it walked east, the war would be followed by a reconciliation. If it walked both east and west, there would be continued hostility, but no actual fighting. If it perked up its ears and barked at the sun, peace was at hand.

Our political analysts pride themselves as "insiders"; in India, the dog was valued because it was so far removed from the corridors of power, even from the norms of life. The Indian dog is the consummate outsider: It stays awake at night, watching, and sleeps in the day. It can be man's "best friend" or turn suddenly rabid. Contrary to the dietary laws, it eats anything. (A common name for dogs in India was "vomit-eater.") Transgressing the restrictions of caste, it has sex indiscriminately with any other dog, and thus is itself the product of miscegenation, a sign of the lowest castes. And it frequently inhabits the cremation grounds, the nowhere land between life and death, where it feeds on carrion.

In India, the dog was trusted and prized for its opinions precisely because of its independence. It was tied to no leash, and it never had lunch with the king.

[1996]

HONG KONG TO MARRY KING KONG

Every night at midnight, Hong Kong television rebroadcasts the evening news program from the mainland, forcing one to rethink Ezra Pound's "news that stays news" as a definition of poetry. This is news that has remained the same for decades. There are scenes of enormous assemblies of elderly men, half of them in military uniforms. Next there is a long series of handshakes: men in brown suits in brown rooms greeting each other or the far taller visiting dignitaries, at least one of whom is an African in an incongruous dashiki. Then the reports from the provinces: an adult literacy class, shiny machines in a new factory, thousands building a bridge or road, a playing field of exercising youth. Each report features an overly extended interview with a single smiling beneficiary.

This being Hong Kong television, the mainland news is interrupted, often, with local commercials. These are not only in a different language (Cantonese or English); they seem to emanate from another world. The half-dressed, sickly models for Calvin Klein mumble about their life-style choices; chirpy newlyweds buy their first bed, winking; women in bikinis slither and lounge; candy-bar chomping teenagers skateboard; naked women shower with their brand of shampoo.

At another midnight soon (June 30), the plodding news will flatten the hyperactive commercials. Yet the extraordinary thing is that nearly everyone I talked to in Hong Kong—rich and poor, business people and intellectuals—believes the opposite: that the Politburo will turn into Calvin Klein; that Hong Kong, in effect, is taking over China. At the least, they told me—one after another, in the identical stock response—China will never kill the golden goose. No one seemed to recall the end of the fable.

Hong Kong has already obliterated its past: unlike the rest of the former British Empire, only a few colonial buildings remain. In its place it has constructed a city of the future: enormous skyscrapers that dwarf New York's, prosperous masses pouring from mall to mall on walkways suspended over unmoving traffic, every other person in animated conversation with a cellular phone. But it is a monument to the future in the one place whose future is so imminently uncertain.

Neither a bestowal of self-rule by a colonial power, nor a revolution or a military conquest, this radical change of government is unprecedented. Without bothering to ask the citizens, Britain, weary of foreign dependents and eager to service the mainland's billion consumers, has decided to honor a treaty made with the Ch'ing Empire and "return" what may be the least regulated yet orderly society on earth to one of the most regulated, and certainly the most volatile. The consequences are impossible to extrapolate.

The agreement, fifteen years in the making, is for what Deng Xiaoping has called "one country, two systems," as though such a thing had proved historically possible. Hong Kong will supposedly become a Special Administrative Region (SAR) of China for the next fifty years, with its own currency, passports, legislature, economy, trade. But there is nothing binding in the agreement—China has already announced its intention to ignore the human rights provisions—and one need only recall that poor devastated Tibet is also a SAR.

No one in China knows what will happen after Deng, now ninety-two, dies. It is merely a coincidence that the handover of Hong Kong is occurring at a moment when urban China is following so enthusiastically his free trade, semi-capitalist road. Many in Hong Kong and in the West assume that the lure of profit from both business and political corruption will keep the country fixed on this path. But China has traditionally opened and closed to the West and, when the center has become shaky, it has usually found that the surest way to unite its people is through nationalism and its concomitant anti-foreign hysteria.

The British and the Chinese have jointly drafted the so-called Basic Law that will govern the SAR—subject to later revision. But surprisingly few of the details of ordinary life have been worked out. A public school principal told me that he doesn't know what changes will be ordered for next year's curriculum, what textbooks he'll be required to use, or even what the school holidays will be. Foreign workers—including over 100,000 Philippine women who work as domestics—have no idea of their future status, what papers they'll need, whether they'll be allowed to remain. Non-Chinese Hong Kong citizens—among them the Indians who have been there since the colony was established in 1842—will become stateless, as will a number of exiled Chinese dissidents. The entire class of civil servants, 40,000 strong, doesn't know if it will have a job in a few months. And reportedly the most terrified subgroup, the prisoners, wait for the imposition of the infamous Chinese penal system and the probable introduction of capital punishment.

One walks in the city and sees questions, large and small, at every step. The Queen's Road—when will they rename the streets? A Protestant church—will it be permitted? A mother with three children—will they implement the one-child policy? Hong Kong drives on the left, China drives on the right. Signs are in English and Chinese—what will happen to English? The Chinese is written in traditional characters; the mainland uses simplified characters—how will they write their own language? And what will their language be? In Hong Kong, the people speak Cantonese, and the bureaucracy is conducted in English; but the national language of China is Mandarin, which few in Hong Kong know well, if at all.*

Hong Kong is too rich to be touched, they kept telling me, illogically: Hong Kong is not Tibet. Though the two have nearly nothing in common, there is one similarity. Few outsiders realize that Hong Kong is as large as it is (399 square miles) and so largely uninhabited (75% of the people occupy 4% of the land). Unlike other cities, Hong Kong expanded by building vertically, creating the most densely populated city

---

* The problem is even more complicated. The regional versions of Chinese are as different from one another as the Romance languages, yet they are all written the same (though pronounced differently). The system worked for the thousands of years in which literacy was the domain of a small educated elite. Now, of course, literacy is almost universal, and as the spoken languages naturally evolve in various directions, there is no way for writing to account for these changes. They don't have the characters. Thus realist novels of Hong Kong street life have dialogue written in Mandarin—as if Raymond Chandler characters had to speak German.

on earth—and yet one can spend an afternoon hiking or col-
lecting seashells on a deserted beach, without another human
in sight. In places it seems as remote as Tibet. But Tibet, since
1959, has been filling with hundreds of thousands of Han
Chinese who will, as is intended, dilute and permanently alter
the culture.

Hong Kong and its lucre will undoubtedly provoke
waves of immigrants from the mainland, legal and illegal, and
there is plenty of room for them. There is already talk of for-
mally joining the city to the Shenzhen Special Economic Zone,
the clone that was created across the border in 1982, and barely populated Lantau island, near the future airport, is likely to
become the first frontier settlement. These new immigrants,
unlike their predecessors during the Great Leap Forward and
the Cultural Revolution, will not be seeking refuge and fortune in a foreign, albeit Chinese, land where they have to
adjust to a new system and new rules. For the next wave,
Hong Kong will simply be another city in China, and they will
bring with them mainland values, connections, and ways of
doing things, and no memory of what life was like in the city
before.

Hong Kongers are notoriously omnivorous: kangaroo
flanks, holothurians, snakes, bamboo fungi, bird's-nests, bear
paws, pig muscles, deer tongues. A few months before the end
of this banquet, they see the People's Liberation Army coming, the new police commissioners, the bureaucrats and
administrators, and think that the changes will merely bring
new platters to the table. They're dreaming, and I was
shocked to find how many share this dream. It will take a few
years, but at best these new colonialists will demand their
share of the spoils of this peace. At worst, they could, with a
sweep of an arm, send the plates crashing. Beijing, old and
modern, has certainly done it before. Meanwhile Hong Kong
is one of the strangest places on earth: an utterly peaceful city
where daily life may or may not radically change in only a few
months in ways that no one knows.

[February 1, 1997]

VOMIT

Out of sheer boredom, Kafka notes in his diary, he washed his hands five times in a row. He lived in the age before MTV. Now the bored, the depressed, the tired, the blank, and the slightly ill can stare at an unending series of rapidly flashing, strange and arresting images, with people who are far more attractive than those who show up in one's dreams. (Why bother to sleep?) Yesterday's transgression is today's decor: MTV is *Un Chien Andalou* at the speed of light, and on a corporate budget: a cabinet of curiosities the size of Xanadu.

Out of sheer boredom, and with clean hands, I turned on MTV twice in recent months, and both times was disappointed to find that the staccato dreamtime of the videos had been replaced by linear and conventional programs. The first was a comedy show, featuring an unremarkably pretty young woman as a lawyer. She walks into a conference room of suited yuppies, male and female, sitting at a long polished table, and immediately vomits at such length and so copiously that it covers the entire table. Unfazed, her colleagues proceed to pluck out pieces with their fingers, which they identify as the remains of certain dishes from various elegant restaurants. (We watched no more that afternoon.)

A few nights later, I stared again, this time at their annual self-celebration, *The MTV Awards*. Sex, dancing, or having a good time—once as intrinsic to rock & roll as amplification and the double entendre—seemed to have dropped out entirely. The main topic was mutability: lachrymose tributes to rap stars who had been murdered in the last year and unhappy humorous references to the fact that almost none of the stars present had been known a year ago, and would undoubtedly be forgotten by next year. The secondary topic was excreta: a popular group of slinky women singers was introduced sitting on toilets, and the vomit jokes, all unmemorable, were relentless. I soon began to notice vomit everywhere; far more vomit on television, in movies, or the latest novels, than one normally sees on the sidewalks outside of bars.

The simpler explanation is that MTV, like all popular culture, is oppressed on two sides. Images are quickly depleted and must be ceaselessly replenished for a listless and sated, largely adolescent audience that demands more outrage. Extravagance, however, is severely constricted by the ecosystem of morality that governs American television: the small packs of the divinely directed who prey on the legislators (who must camouflage themselves with forceful positions on uncontroversial issues in order to be reelected) and the corporations (whose advertisements feed television and therefore must attract as many potential customers as possible, repelling none). Sex, on MTV, in this tension of attraction and repulsion, has essentially reached its limit of innuendo. To maintain its allure of the forbidden, of taboos being broken, and to keep the kids from changing the channel, the station must rely on equally fascinating, if less appealing, bodily functions—aspects of the body to which the moralists are oddly indifferent.

[A digression: In the U.S., moral issues, particularly concerning the "corruption" of youth, are inextricably entwined with physical health. The 19th century was the era of apostles of strenuous exercise as a means for keeping youth from bad thoughts and deeds. (Today, of course, the muscled body is presumed to have more frequent contact with other, equally muscled, bodies.) In the 1950's, the main corrupter of children was believed—thanks to a best-selling book called *Seduction of the Innocent* by Dr. Frederick Wertham—to be comic books. This intersected with the polio epidemic to create a myth that the disease was being spread by comics; there were mass burnings around the country. More recently, the morally enlightened have ascribed the spread of a virus to the "pornography" of television and popular music. Conversely, whenever youth is involved, health issues are treated as moral questions, most notably in the cases of AIDS and drugs.]

The more complicated explanation for this manifestation of the half-digested is that ever since youth detached itself from adult society, shortly after the Second World War, and became a separate but parallel culture, it has been a reliable indicator of the society at large. Its exaggerated responses and actions are not only canaries in our coal mines, but often extreme versions of what are or will soon be norms. Vomit has become an adolescent preoccupation, not only as entertainment, but as obsession: a prevailing psychological disorder among teenage girls in the technological countries. Bulimia is a response that is both violent and reasonable: In this society, what else can one do but throw up?

For the last twenty-five years, those who are not poor in the First World have been under siege by armies of production. In the arts alone, the record stores carry hundreds of thousands of CD's; the video store on my corner has forty thousand films; my local television has seventy channels; the *Directory of American Poets* lists some seven thousand poets, all reputedly alive and publishing; there's a web site that sells a million new books and another with ten million out-of-print ones; the number of art galleries, theater and dance and music companies in any large city inspires one to stay home and contemplate the void. The other day I wanted some information on a writer who died ten years ago: the library had two hundred full-length critical studies and thousands of articles; an Internet search listed seven thousand web sites where the writer's name appeared. I decided to direct my curiosity elsewhere, and tried to remember someone who had been completely forgotten.

One result of this excess of all things is that if you are a fanatic of any given subject—let us say, poetry or movies—it is more than likely that your fellow enthusiast has not read the same books or seen the same films. You have nothing to talk about together. This lack of a shared knowledge or a common ground—not of a "tradition," but of a sense of the contemporary, of what is being produced right now, to advocate, modify, or oppose—is unprecedented. It is perhaps the one thing, beyond the gadgets, that is genuinely new.

This means, in the arts, that it is nearly impossible to have any impact. The first edition of *The Waste Land* was only five hundred copies, but it transformed poetry in various languages, and was known, whether adulated or rejected, by all readers of modern poetry. This has become unimaginable: the last book to have an immediate international effect on literature at large, *One Hundred Years of Solitude*, occurred thirty years ago, just before this Age of Proliferation.

It also means, for the maker of art, that to produce implies a conscious decision not to consume, if only momentarily—to arrogantly proclaim one's right or need to ceremoniously place one's tiny little leaf in this rain forest. In the general population, the feeling of helplessness amidst the multiplication of humanity and its products has, among other things, led to the creation of group identities, which are not only assertions of community and self in the collapsing of traditional societal units, but also a way, however inadvertent, to keep one's consumerism on a human scale. Religious affiliation, in its stricter forms, neatly parcels much of the world into acceptable and taboo. Monolithic advocates of ethnic or sexual identities can happily concern themselves with the work of confederates and remain unashamedly oblivious of others. Intended—in their constructive aspects—to erase the worst forms of provincialism, group identities seek the refuge of a new provincialism in a cosmopolitanized world: a dream of an orderly and focused life, where one knows what one wants to discover and know.

The rest of us can only stuff ourselves and vomit and stuff ourselves again. This is not the banquet vomiting of the Romans, which was a kind of potlatch: a demonstration of one's wealth or power through the greatest possible display of waste. This is a guilty vomiting, the vomiting of a bulimic, who may well be the emblem of the age.

In the psychological studies, the bulimia of teenage girls is generally seen as a self-destructive response to perceptions of inadequacy (*I am stupid, ugly, fat*); shame (*my family is poor; I've been sexually abused*); and failure (*I am bad at school, making friends, meeting boys . . .*); as well as a strategy of avoidance (*. . . therefore I won't try*). With a slight translation, these are the feelings of nearly everyone in the hyper-production of the West: *I have consumed too many things; I can't possibly keep up with all the things to consume; I'm always consuming the wrong thing; I'm too stupid or uninformed to know which thing to consume; I've consumed too many of the wrong things; there are too many things so I won't consume any. . . .* The Western consumer lives in the guilt of excess, the dizziness of choices, the identification of self through one's selections (in current spoken

American, one way to say "I like spaghetti" is "I am a spaghetti person"), the doubts about one's self as seen through one's selections, the continual belief that one has made the wrong choice (brand of VCR, color of wall paint, sofa, lover or spouse) when there are so many others.

The allure of the mass media has always been the presentation of what we are not and would like to be: leading lives of wealth, adventure, and passion. The images of vomiting that appear as one nervously clicks the remote control are not only there as bizarre novelties to make us pause at a certain channel and its commercials. They are there because we wish we could clear a space, make some room, expunge all the half-digested matter in our brains, stop for a moment the interminable consumption and its attendant anxieties, know again the feeling of hunger and the feeling of satisfaction. We look at people throwing up because we wish we could throw it all up—including these images of people throwing up.

[1997]

TEETH

"To write about teeth. Just try."
—Elias Canetti

I had a pet rabbit who developed a dental problem. Her upper and lower incisors did not meet to grind each other down, and they kept growing. If left unattended, as sometimes happens in the wild, the teeth will grow to such length that they curve back into the rabbit's skull and pierce the brain. The veterinarian told me to buy a pair of special podiatrist's scissors and regularly clip her teeth.

The first time I tried, I botched the job. The teeth shattered; there was blood. An hour later I had to take a plane to another country, to attend one of those cultural conventions, always held abroad, where foreign governments treat otherwise obscure intellectuals to exorbitant hospitality.

I was met at the airport by an official, ushered to the front of the immigration line, and taken in a limousine to an elegant hotel. That night, in a suite on the fortieth floor, looking over the radiant expanse of the enormous city, marooned in the vastness of a bed designed for a free-love ashram, I couldn't sleep. The memory of the rabbit's bloody mouth kept me staring.

The next morning another limousine took me, a French poet, and a Chinese painter for a visit to a provincial capital. I already knew the place, so while the others toured the cathedral, I went to find a junk store on the Street of Frogs where, years before, I had bought a small, rusty mechanical device whose function no one has ever been able to ascertain.

Walking the colonial streets, I came across a crowd of a few hundred people and some television crews milling about, apparently waiting for something. I had read in the local paper that students had been protesting some university action; I assumed that the crowd was expecting a demonstration to march by. Half of the block was deserted. The people on either side had formed their own barriers, in order, I thought, to keep the sight lines clear for the cameras. There were no police, no agitation, nothing more than the familiar sight of a large group in the semi-comatose state of idle expectation.

A tourist, I was following a map, and my map told me that the shortest distance to where I was going was across the no man's land of the empty half-block. I walked along the sidewalk unhurriedly. People on either side began waving frantically, perhaps, I thought, because I was stumbling into what was to be the television picture. Then there was the crack of a shot, and I saw the brick wall a few inches from my head chip. Unalarmed, barely registering the event, not reacting with the "fight or flight" supposedly programmed in the genes, I quickened my pace, but did not run, toward the crowd on the other side. The next day I read that a student group was occupying the building; a rival group was trying to take it from them; the first group had placed snipers on the roof; two people had been shot that day.

The rabbit was all right. Her teeth resumed growing, and I periodically clipped with increasing expertise. I suddenly developed asthma, and tests showed that I was violently allergic to rabbits; but the rabbit stayed on: what else could I do, eat it? One night the following summer, at a house in the country, a Siberian husky belonging to a neighbor smashed through the small cage where the rabbit was living, mauled her to death, and then couldn't get out.

I thought of my pet rabbit a few years later, after reading a review of a book of mine in an academic journal. It ended: "Weinberger simply needs a freshman English class." The critic had been, considering his other remarks, uncharacteristically perceptive on this point. I had never had a freshman English class, having spent those years on the adolescent version of contemplating the void. So, in the American spirits of self-improvement and self-reliance, I decided to give myself some lessons, and assigned myself an essay on a favorite pet; it seemed the thing to do.

I sent it to an old friend, a writer of short fictions who occasionally teaches the writing of short fiction. She thought the composition vague and pointless; if I was trying to draw a parallel between myself and the rabbit as victims, it wasn't very clear. This connection had never occurred to me; I thought I was writing an associative narrative somewhat in the style of Felisberto Hernández, albeit with less charm. Discouraged, I abandoned the essay.

Recently, I came across this challenge from Elias Canetti, the most obstinate of writers, who was, insufferably, always right. There have been notable writers who were doctors, but no writers I can remember who were dentists, although both practice oral arts. The decay of the tooth has never been as moving as the decay of the body. More exactly, the sickness of the tooth and its subsequent extraction have tended to be viewed allegorically rather than as revelatory of human nature. Toothlessness is a political metaphor for powerlessness, and was once a Christian metaphor for the absence of licentiousness; the two combined to become the Freudian dream symbol of castration. Toothache, said Petrarch, is a reminder of death, which is eternal life.

The teeth of my pet rabbit were neither allegorical nor particularly revelatory. She was toothsome, but not powerful; she may well have been licentious, as reputation has it, but she lacked the companionship of her kind. I hope her teeth did not ache, but who can know the aches of a rabbit? As it is said, almost, the heart of a rabbit is a dark forest.

[1995/1998]

THE LAUGHING FISH

In *The Ocean Made of Streams of Story*, the 11th-century Kashmiri precursor to *The Thousand and One Nights* as a vast compendium of nested tales, there is an image that reappears in insomnia. The King sees one of his wives leaning over a balcony and talking to a Brahmin. In a fit of jealousy, he orders the Brahmin to be put to death. As the man is being led through the town to his execution, a fish, lying in a stall in the market, bursts out laughing. The King stops the execution to find out why the fish laughed. (The reason is that the Brahmin is completely innocent, while the harem of the King's dissolute wives is full of men disguised as women . . . but that's another story.)

In a footnote, the annotator of the 1923 edition of the C.H. Tawney translation, the seemingly omniscient N.M. Penzer, M.A., F.R.G.S., F.G.S, cites an article in the 1916 volume of the *Journal of the American Oriental Society* on "Psychic *Motifs* in Hindu Fiction, and the Laugh and Cry *Motif*." Its author, identified only as "Professor Bloomfield," classifies the various kinds of laughter found in that literature: "There is the cry and laugh together, and each separately. Of laughter by itself, there is the laugh of joy, of irony, malice, trickery, and triumph. Then there is the sardonic laugh, the enigmatic, fateful laugh (sometimes with ironic humor in it), and finally there is the laugh of mystery, as in the case of the fish that laughed." The taxonomy seems more human than Hindu, but in any event, the category of mere mystery for the laughing fish is weak.

With the exception of the shark, fish have never been given any human attributes. No fish is as contented as a cow, sly as a fox, wise as an elephant or an owl, industrious as a bee, faithful as a turtledove, self-sacrificing as a pelican, or even as lowly as a worm. Aesop, though he came from a maritime culture, has only one talking fish in his hundreds of fables: an undersized pickerel who tries to persuade the fisherman to throw him back. Without any particular personality, it merely argues for its survival.

Adam doesn't know their names. He is shown all the beasts of the field and the fowls of the air and—the theological questions are unresolvable—either names them (by what process and in what language?) or calls them by the names they already have (which assumes a divine language, now lost, where the signifier was not random). But no fish are hauled up before him in Eden. His ignorance continues on as a blank area in the human brain: the otherwise multilingual often struggle to translate the fish on a menu.

Lawrence, in a celebrated poem in *Birds, Beasts and Flowers*, writes: "Fish, oh Fish,/ So little matters!/. . . To be a fish!// So utterly without misgiving/. . . / Loveless and so lively/ . . . / . . . soundless, and out of contact./ They exchange no word, no spasm, not even anger./ Not one touch./ Many suspended together, forever apart,/ Each one alone with the waters. . . ." The poem takes six pages to say: "They are beyond me, are fishes."

The beyond of the fishes may be why watching them is the most peaceful activity on earth, floating above them with a mask and snorkel. (A public aquarium is contaminated by the presence of the sounds of the other people; an aquarium at home always remains in the context of the other objects of one's life; scuba is inextricable from its respiratory anxiety.) More than merely watching bright-colored creatures dart around, its tranquility comes from its total lack of human association. Fish have no connection to our emotional life: unlike the other creatures, they do not mate (as Lawrence, naturally, keeps repeating), they hardly squabble, they do not care for their young. Even insects work. A fish swims and eats, is pure movement and beauty. It inhabits a world we can only watch weightlessly, soundlessly, and behind glass. To watch fish is to not be oneself. Even in a magnificent landscape, we inhabit that landscape; it is full of smells and sounds and imagery that connect to countless thoughts, feelings, memories, artworks. Standing under a night sky inevitably leads to thoughts of one's significance in the universe. But a fish neither reflects nor questions our existence. A fish is and we are: to become engrossed in watching fish is to forget that we are, but without, as mystics experience, becoming part of what we observe. The world is everything that is not the case. A laughing fish would not only be like us, it would care enough to laugh at us, a terrifying thing.

[1999]

RENGA

The forest

When in Angola, do not enter the forest of the Cokwe at night. For there Muhangi, an old man, once a great hunter, runs through the woods screaming. Kanyali, in the form of a girl, chases wanderers with a termite hill on his head. Kapwakala, a child who lives in the holes of trees, rustles an apron made of hide. There is Ciyeye, a bonfire that walks, and Kalulu, a small red child that whizzes buzzing through the air. Samutambieka, an unknown animal with one foot, one eye, one ear, and one tooth, carries a club red with the blood of humans. And worst of all is Nguza, a large eye that squats on a tree branch and stares.

Blue eyes

I was in a village on the Amazon, waiting day after day for a boat to get me out. I slept in the one place that let rooms; switching on the light at night, the ceiling was covered with hundreds of transparent salamanders, motionless and upside-down. The one place to eat was a windowless shack with an unlit kitchen and two metal tables outside on the dirt road that was the only street. I sat. In one late afternoon of sitting, an elderly man came down the road and spoke to me. "*Sprechen sie Deutsch?*" He wore clean denim clothes faded to the color of clouds, and his face had long been in the sun. Disappointed at my ignorance, he switched to English for his monologue: "You probably think I am an Indian, but I am not an Indian. Look at my eyes, they are blue. Indians do not have blue eyes. I am not an Indian. Indians are like animals. In Germany we had the right idea. One little injection and poof! no more. Look at my eyes, they are blue. . . ." And on and on into the dark.

Most Germans believed that Hitler had blue eyes, but they were brown. The official portrait photographs of high

Nazi officials were often retouched to give them blue eyes and
that particular stare, pure and cold as a mountain lake, as a
glacier, as a cloudless sky, as the fruit of an imaginary
unmixed blood.

Years later, I was in a car driving across a plain in India,
hours from any town, in a monotony of mud-baked villages
with a single tree, two men squatting in the shade of a wall
smoking, three children scratching lines in the dirt, four vul-
tures bickering over the carcass of a dog, a woman leading a
single goat, two men on an oxcart, three crows pecking aim-
lessly, four flies resting on my leg. The car slowed, as was
often, for a herd of cows that filled the road. Walking among
them was a wandering mendicant, with the usual orange
robe, wooden staff, and begging bowl, his shaven head painted with the lines of Shiva. But he was far taller than usual, and
his skin was a burnt pink, not brown. As the car slowly rolled
past him, he raised his bowl to the window, not speaking, and
stared at me for a moment with celestial, incomprehensible,
glacial blue eyes.

Flies

A fly on a window cannot understand how there is a world he
sees but cannot reach. A fly, as it has often been said, on a
piece of shit is in paradise; a fly in honey is doomed. Vishnu's
fly whisk, made of yak hair, signifies the dharma: they are and
we are and we cannot help but flick them away. A fly knows
a pleasure denied to mammals: mating in mid-air. Beelzebub,
the Lord of the Flies. A man who saw like a fly—kaleidoscop-
ically—would go mad; a fly who saw like a man would be
depressed by linearity. Apollonius of Tyana rid Byzantium of
flies by making a bronze fly and burying it under a pillar. A
fly may be thinking of other things, or not thinking; it doesn't
look where it's going, and crashes into a screen. Yoko Ono
filmed a fly climbing a breast like the conquest of Everest.
Russians girls used to carve turnips into coffins and bury flies.
The fly on the man's open wound was merely being a fly,
enjoying the fact that the man was merely human. Charles

Reznikoff, given a job in Hollywood with nothing to do, wrote poems about silence and solitude to the flies on his desk.

A child dreams of himself in the first version of the movie *The Fly*: the tiny human head on the fly's body, trapped in a web, squeaking "Help me." An adult dreams of himself in the second version of the movie *The Fly*: she still loves him no matter how monstrous he has become.

Three sentences on the way to Belize

Sitting in the last row of the plane next to a Belizean woman of uncertain age. The choice for lunch was pasta, fish, or chicken, but by the time the meal cart reached us, there was only pasta or fish. My seatmate smiled sweetly at the stewardess and said, "Next time you'll have to kill more chickens."

A paragraph there

Flung flying down the unpaved and cratered Hummingbird Highway, past the village of Hummingbird, ten houses on stilts. The Hummingbird River flows down from the Hummingbird Mountains, each one of which is called Mt. Hummingbird. It is said the people here have exceptionally small imaginations. They say a woman is as beautiful as a hummingbird, a boy is as quick as a hummingbird, a remark as sharp as a hummingbird's beak, the morning as hazy as hummingbirds' wings, a man as silent as a hummingbird, things are as small as or larger than hummingbirds, and the food is so good a hummingbird might hover over the plate. When a man dies, he is born again as a hummingbird. When a hummingbird dies, it goes to paradise. There it lives forever in the village of Hummingbird, by the Hummingbird River, under the Hummingbird Mountains. Everything is the same, except that there is no Hummingbird Highway, for there's no place else to go.

The wings of angels

The soul is often represented as a bird and angels have wings because life occurs here and the afterlife is somewhere up there. But a corpse in most cultures is laid on its back, and gravity pulls the fluids down, giving the upper sections their waxy pallor. The lower sections darken as the blood settles, except in those places where the body is touching the surface on which it is laid. There, the pressure of the weight of the corpse pushes the blood from the tissue, forming areas that are much lighter than the rest. One of those areas is across the shoulder blades and upper back, and it takes the form of perfectly symmetrical wings.

America: the dead

People die, but there are no dead in America. The dead are those who are exhumed a year after burial, their bones washed and placed in catacombs or in a special niche in the house, their skulls painted, with jewels set in the eye sockets, their skulls set on spikes around the yard. The dead are those buried in suits of jade to live forever, with the ornaments, weapons, cooking utensils, and food they'll need in the other world. The dead are buried sitting on a chair, facing east. The dead have a rooster carved on their gravestones, to announce the soul's awakening. The dead are the ones for whom incense, candles, paper money, paper cars, paper houses with paper dishwashers and VCR's are burnt. The dead are the ones whose memorial tablets and portraits occupy a prominent place in the living room or in the temple. The dead have graves that are visited with regularity and kept from weeds, or inspire melancholy at their abandonment. The dead have graves where the family picnics once a year and misbehaves. The dead inhabit a place where the living, through chants or trance or solitude or drugs, can talk to them. The dead are those who take possession of the living. The dead are those who come back.

There are no dead in America because there are no corpses. Corpses are the invisible citizens of America, the secret no one tells, far rarer to observe by chance than copulation. We don't see them, we don't touch them, we don't dress them, we don't know what to do with them, we don't keep them in our bedrooms until they are interred, we don't watch their feet sticking out from the shroud as the flames consume them. So many people die on television in America because in our lives no one dies, they only vanish, and television is the great compensator for all we don't have or see.

There are no dead in America because there is no place. The dead are dependent on generations that do not move. The dead have graves where the family knows where the graves are. In America the ancestors are left behind in a nation constructed, like no other, on the pursuit of happiness, a dream of the future where the dead have no place. There is no happiness to pursue among the dead. The country was settled (in its historical era) as an escape from the dead. Except for those who came in the early years to practice their religion—to maintain the old ways—its emigrants have come seeking freedom from the tyranny of the dead and, like released slaves, they must wander and invent themselves. The generations move on, new people, forever "making a new start," holding the ethical ideal of being "born again" in this life.

In the dream of no history, small fears fester and infect. The standard American horror movie plot is the house, the school, the mall built over a forgotten cemetery, and the subsequent revenge of the desecrated: a story unimaginable anywhere else. Visiting the United States in 1944, the Chinese anthropologist Fei Tsao-t'ung reported that "people move about like the tide, unable to form permanent ties with places, to say nothing of other people. . . . Naturally they seldom see ghosts."

A report from Salcombe Regis, Devon

John Bastone, dairyman, baptized 30th March 1817, writes:
"About 120 years ago, the ghost of a Mr. Lyde appeared in the orchard on the east side of the road running along the foot of Salcombe Hill. (The orchard is numbered 561 in the Ordnance Survey map of the district.)

"Every year the ghost advanced a cock-stride nearer to Sid House, until, at last, it sat on a gate on the opposite side of the road. (The gate led into a field numbered 553 on the Ordnance Survey map.)

"Then, still at the incredibly slow pace of a cock-stride a year, he proceeded to an old oak tree almost in the centre of the field. This oak tree, although a bit battered by the storms of many years, is still to be seen standing in the meadow.

"After many more years, the determined spectre arrived in the cellar of Sid House. A maid-servant, on going to the cellar to fetch liquor, saw the ghost of Mr. Lyde sitting on a barrel, eating bread and cheese, with a quart of cider beside him.

"Eventually, to the horror and dismay of the people living in the house, the ghost, with a look of triumph, sat down to dinner with them one night.

"The family decided that to share the table during their evening meal with an apparition was more than they could bear, so one of them rode to Mr. George Cornish of Pascombe in the Harcombe Valley, to ask him if he would come and try to lay the obstinate ghost.

"Mr. Cornish arrived, carrying with him a small Bible, and with very little difficulty laid the spectre."

The Hidden Span

The Taoist universe is an infinity of nested cycles of time, each revolving at a different pace, and those who are not mere mortals pertain to different cycles. Certain teachings take 400 years to transmit from sage to student; others, 4,000; others, 40,000. It is said that Lao-tzu, the author of the *Tao Te Ching*, spent 81 years in the womb.

Taoist ritual begins with the construction of an altar that is a calendar and a map of this universe. At its perimeter, twenty-four pickets, the Twenty-Four Energy Nodes, each representing fifteen days, to form a year of 360 days. Within, a proliferation of markers for the Two Principles (yin and yang), the Three Energies, the Three Irrational Powers, the Five Elements, the Five Tones, the Six Rectors, the Eight

Trigrams and Sixty-Four Hexagrams of the *I Ching*, the Nine Palaces and the Nine Halls, the Ten Stems, the Twelve Branches. . . Each is a supernatural being, a gate, a direction, a part of the body, a measurement of time, a philosophical concept, an alchemical substance. As Lao-tzu said, "The Tao created one, one gave birth to two, two to three, and three to the ten thousand things."

Typically of Taoism, this system has an inherent flaw: a hole in time, called the Irrational Opening. If, at a certain moment, which is always changing, one walks backward through the various gates in a certain order, one can escape time and enter the Hidden Span. In this other time beyond all the other times, one finds oneself in the holy mountains; there one can gather healing herbs, magic mushrooms, and elixirs that bring immortality.

The technique was first taught to the Yellow Emperor by the six calendrical Jade Maidens, who in turn learned it from the Mysterious Woman of the Nine Heavens, also known as the Lady of the Ultimate Yin. Its most famous practitioner was a very real military strategist, Chu-ko Liang (181–234). To repel an invading army, he placed hidden markers on an enormous plain to secretly replicate a Taoist altar, and then tricked the troops into entering through a certain symbolic gate. Although the landscape appeared unremarkable, the army found itself trapped in a labyrinth of an alternate time from which it could not escape.

Angola

When in Angola, do not enter the forest, or the fields, or walk by the side of the roads, or walk along the many roads that have been untraveled for years. There are fifteen million land mines buried there: East German PPM-2's that were once an invisible wall beyond the Wall; Chinese 72-A's, made largely of plastic so the metal detectors cannot find them, with anti-handling devices to prevent their removal; Romanian MAI-75's, a half of a grapefruit in size, with a thick slice of cyclonite, the mixture of TNT and RDX; American "spiders" that are dropped from planes and send out a web of trip wires when they land; green camouflaged plastic Soviet "butter-flies" that flutter down from helicopters, or are fired from mortars, and cannot be disarmed. It takes a hundred men two days to clear a patch of land the size of a soccer field; in Angola, most of the arable land is unapproachable. There are villages that have been trapped in total isolation for more than a decade; their stories still unknown.

[1999]

III

MACDIARMID

"My job," he wrote, is "to erupt like a volcano, emitting not only flame, but a lot of rubbish." Heat, fireworks, acrid smoke, and tons of dead ash are indeed among his attributes, but a volcano is too small a trope for Hugh MacDiarmid. He occupied—perhaps he was himself—an entire planet.

"Hugh MacDiarmid": the dominant pseudonym among a dozen pseudonyms and one actual birth-name, Christopher Murray Grieve. They wrote about each other, usually in praise, sometimes in disagreement. They were Nietzschean Marxist Christians; supporters of Mussolini and Stalin and Scottish nationalism; followers of Hindu Vedanta. They produced tens of thousands of pages of journalism and commissioned books, edited anthologies and a string of magazines; wrote an autobiography estimated to be 4,000 pages long, hundreds of pages of fiction and translations, hundreds of letters to editors and thousands to friends and enemies, and, above all, some 2,000 pages of poetry, much of it in long lines. They wrote in variations of two languages, with passages in a few dozen others, even Norn. One of the two primary languages, "synthetic Scots," was their own invention. And behind the curtains of this vast collective enterprise was a short, often miserable and alcoholic man, a nationalist who hated his nation, a gregarious misanthrope who spent most of his life in extreme poverty. All of his teeth were extracted at 24; most of his writing was completed by 50; he died at 86 and never learned to type: MacDiarmid!

The work that will survive begins in 1922, when, at age 30, Christopher Grieve gave birth to Hugh MacDiarmid. At the time he was a nine-to-five journalist for small-town newspapers and a bad Georgian English poet. Most of the passions of his life were already in place: Scottish nationalism, which was flaring around him, lit by the Irish and Russian revolutions; Marxism; the Social Credit schemes of Major C.H. Douglas, championed by A.R. Orage and Ezra Pound in the *New Age*.

95

His heroes were Nietzsche and Lenin ("I have no use for anything between genius and the working man"), Dostoyevsky
for his nationalist spiritualism, and the Russian philosopher
Leo Shestov for his evocation of the limitlessness of the imagination, an imagination beyond all dogmas, and where all
contradictions are reconciled.

For Scottish writers at the time, the central question was
what language to write. Middle Scots, in the 15th and 16th
centuries, had been one of the grand vehicles for poetry: the
Great Makars Robert Henrysoun and William Dunbar (whom
the English call the "Scottish Chaucerians"), Gawin Douglas'
magnificent version of the *Aeneid*, Mark Alexander Boyd's single and perfect sonnet, "Venus and Cupid." After 1603—the
death of Queen Elizabeth, the transformation of the Scottish
James VI into the English James I, and the subsequent loss of
Scottish autonomy in the "United Kingdom"—Scots as a literary language decayed. In the 18th century, Allan Ramsay,
Robert Fergusson, and finally Robert Burns attempted a
revival that never quite caught on. (Their greatest contemporary, David Hume, for one, spoke Scots in private but wrote
only in English.) Ironically, it was the success of Burns that
strangled the movement: Scots became the domain of the
corny songs of his imitators, which in turn led to vaudeville
parodies. By the time of Grieve's childhood, kids were pun-
ished for speaking Scots in school; it was considered unspeakably vulgar.

There was a new Scots Revival movement, led by the various Burns Societies, which Grieve and his pseudonyms had
violently opposed as reactionary and irrelevant to the struggle. But by 1922, the wonder year of Modernism, a conjunction of forces changed his mind. His mentor, the militant
nationalist Lewis Spence (now remembered as an historian of
Atlantis) suddenly switched sides and supported Scots. There
were the examples of the revival of Gaelic in the Irish
Republic and the invention of Nynorsk, a new language created out of various rural dialects, which became the official
second language of Norway. There were the writings by
Gregory Smith promoting the idea of a unique Scottish psychological make-up: the Caledonian Antisyzygy, capable of

holding "without conflict irreconcilable opinions," "easily passing from one mood to the other," and with a "zest for handling a multiple of details"—a perfect description, in fact, of MacDiarmid himself. Moreover, there was the general belief that this sensibility—anticipating, in a way, Benjamin Lee Whorf's studies of the Hopi—could only be expressed by the Scots language. ("Speakin' o' Scotland in English words," MacDiarmid later wrote, was like "Beethoven chirpt by birds.") And most of all, there were the examples of Charles Doughty and James Joyce: Doughty, mining his poems from archaic English, and Joyce, opening the gates for all the world's languages to rush in. From them, Grieve believed that one's spoken language was not enough, that one must ransack the dictionaries for precision of expression.

Grieve created MacDiarmid—and kept MacDiarmid's identity secret for years—as an experiment in writing in Scots. His goal was to return not to the folkish Burns, but to the continental and intellectual Dunbar; to "extend the Vernacular to embrace the whole range of modern culture," as well as to delineate the Scottish mind. By doing so, he thought he would help to sever Scotland from England and insert it into Europe as a nation among equals.

His sources were books like John Jamieson's 1808 *Etymological Dictionary of the Scottish Language* and Sir James Wilson's *Lowland Scotch as Spoken in the Lower Strathearn District of Perthshire*. There he found the words like *watergaw* (an indistinct rainbow) and *yow-trummle* (cold weather in July after sheep-shearing) and *peerieweerie* (dwindled to a thread of sound) that would fill the lyrics of his first important books, *Sangschaw* (1925) and *Penny Wheep* (1926). As one stumbles through these poems now, the eyes bouncing between the lines and the glossary below, it is important to remember that this is exactly how most Scottish readers would have had to read it at the time. (Worse, the glossaries in those early editions were in the back.) MacDiarmid's Scots—and later, much of his English—are written in a language foreign to everyone.

From these early short pieces, which he later dismissed as "chocolate boxes," he set out to write the Scots *Ulysses* or *The Waste Land*, a poem that could demonstrate that Scots was not only a medium for lyrics, but also for the rigorous intellect of difficult "modern" works. The result was *A Drunk Man Looks at the Thistle* (1926), a poem five times as long as Eliot's. Like *The Waste Land*, which makes a cameo appearance in the poem, it is written in a variety of styles and meters—though largely interspersed among ballad stanzas—and it collages other texts: translations of whole poems by Alexander Blok and Else Lasker-Schüler, and some forgotten continentals such as Zinaida Hippius, George Ramaekers, and Edmond Rocher, to give the poem a European context. Like "Prufrock" it is an interior monologue, though one that continually locates itself. To *Ulysses'* single day, it takes place in a single night; its Molly is Jean, who similarly has the last word. Its narrative comes from Burns' "Tam o' Shanter," who was also on his way home from the taverns at midnight, and its inspiration from Paul Valery's *La Jeune Parque*, which the French poet described as "the transformation of a consciousness in the course of one night."

    A Drunk Man is unquestionably the Scots masterpiece of the century, and nearly all of MacDiarmid's critics and acolytes consider it his greatest work. Certainly it is dense with complexities that are still being unraveled in a parade of monographs, most of them written in Scotland. But it is a curious late Symbolist work in the age of High Modernism. The thistle itself is fraught with significant meaning, and would have appalled the Imagists: emblem of Scotland and the Scottish character, sign of the Drunk Man's virility, image of the soul flowering over the thorns of the "miseries and grandeurs of human fate"; it even becomes Ygdrasil, the cosmic tree. And its Nietzschean narrative has dated badly: the triumph of the intellect and the soul over drunkenness, psychological difficulties, cultural inferiorities, and doubt; the dream of the transformation of the low-born Drunken Man, the poet, into "A greater Christ, a greater Burns"—an odd pair as models for one's superior self. At the end of a century that has seen what can be wrought by acts of "the beautiful violent will," it is MacDiarmid's Nietzscheism more than his Stalinism—perhaps they are the same—that is most difficult to take.

Though *A Drunk Man* sold poorly, Hugh MacDiarmid became the most famous poet in Scotland, and Grieve and the pseudonyms shrank in his shadow (except of course when writing articles about him). In the 1920's he edited three magazines, including *The Scottish Chapbook*, which is considered to be the greatest Scottish literary review ever, and contributed to dozens of magazines with "Scots" or "Scottish" in their titles; founded the Scottish chapter of PEN; joined and broke with countless political organizations; stood for Parliament a few times; and held posts in local governments like Convener of Parks and Gardens, Hospitalmaster, member of the Water Board. A hero-worshiper, he read the news from Italy and—as many did at the time—mistook National Socialism for socialism and wrote "A Plea for Scottish Fascism." But his continuing loyalty was to Lenin and Major Douglas and Dostoyevsky ("This Christ o' the neist thoosand years"), believing that the combination of Marxist-Leninism and Social Credit would end the struggle for material existence and prepare the world for the struggle for spiritual transcendence.

In 1933, at age 41, he went into a kind of exile and a prodigious burst of writing perhaps unmatched by any other writer in the century. With his wife, Valda Trevlyn, and son Michael, he moved to a place called Sodom on the tiny island of Whalsay in the Shetlands, paying two shillings a month for a house without electricity and water a quarter of a mile away. The family subsisted on gifts of fish and potatoes from their neighbors and gulls' eggs gathered in the cliffs. In his eight years there, MacDiarmid wrote a series of hack-works, with titles like *Scottish Doctors, Scottish Eccentrics, The Islands of Scotland, Scottish Scene*; political tracts like *Red Scotland, or What Lenin Has Meant to Scotland* and *Scotland and the Question of a Popular Front Against Fascism and War*; and an autobiography estimated to be a million words long, parts of which were later published as *Lucky Poet* and *The Company I've Kept*. He edited a series of books on Scotland and a large anthology of Scottish poetry, translating the Gaelic sections himself, in collaboration with Sorley Maclean. He was expelled from the National Party of Scotland for Communism and from the Communist Party for nationalism. He had a nervous breakdown and was hospitalized for some months. And there was more:

He set out to write, in English, the longest poem ever written by one individual, *Cornish Heroic Song for Valda Trevlyn*. In the two years between 1937 and 1939, he wrote some six or seven hundred pages of it—one third of the intended whole. This was virtually all of the poetry (with the exception of *The Battle Continues*), largely unrevised, that he was to publish for the next forty years.

The *Cornish Heroic Song* has never been reconstructed. According to MacDiarmid's biographer, Alan Bold, the first part was a 20,000-line section entitled *Mature Art*. MacDiarmid sent a 10,000-line version to Eliot at Faber's, which the poet admired (while finding the title "forbidding"), but the publisher rejected. Of the surviving longer poems, "In Memoriam James Joyce" (now 150 pages in the so-called *Complete Poems*) was originally merely a piece of *Mature Art*. "The Kind of Poetry I Want" (now fifty pages) was to run throughout the *Cornish Heroic Song*, and "Direadh" (now thirty pages) was to be in a later section. It is unclear where all the other poems belonged, and "Cornish Heroic Song for Valda Trevlyn" itself now survives as an eight-page poem. In 1967 MacDiarmid published a book of poetry called *A Lap of Honour*, containing, he claimed, poems that had been omitted from his 1962 *Collected* because he'd forgotten that he'd written them. Rescued by the scholar Duncan Glen, these contained some of his greatest works, including "Diamond Body" and "Once in a Cornish Garden."

Various forces impel the poems of *Cornish Heroic Song*: First, the attempt to create a "synthetic English," as he had invented a "synthetic Scots," a project inspired by Doughty, but with a vocabulary drawn not, as Doughty had done, from archaicisms, but from the new language of science. It is a poetry of "hard facts," of hundreds of thousands of details ("The universal *is* the particular"), and its ultimate mysticism anticipates the computer age, where an unprecedented precision of measurement and description has only made the universe far more mysterious.

Second, MacDiarmid discovered that the way out of the traditional prosody and rhyme he had hitherto employed almost exclusively was to break prose down into long jagged lines. Often this meant transcribing—the current term is "sampling"—other people's prose: long passages from obscure travel and science books, reviews in *The Times Literary Supplement*, Herman Melville's letters, Martin Buber, Thomas Mann's "Tonio Kröger." His practice of reproducing these uncredited led to charges of plagiarism later in his life, but plagiarism, to his mind, was beside the point for an epic that was to include everything.

Third, he had come to believe that the poetry of the classless society was not the personal lyric, but an epic without heroes (or with thousands of heroes). And he had taken to heart the words of Lenin's last speech, delivered in 1922 in a prose that sounds like MacDiarmid's, and which are quoted twice in *Lucky Poet*:

> It would be a very serious mistake to suppose that one can become a Communist without making one's own the treasures of human knowledge . . . . Communism becomes an empty phrase, a mere façade, and the Communist a mere bluffer, if he has not worked over in his consciousness the whole inheritance of human knowledge—made his own and worked over anew all that was of value in the more than two thousand years [!] of development of human thought.

The result, then, was, in MacDiarmid's words, "an enormous poem,"

> dealing with the interrelated themes of the evolution of world literature and world consciousness, the problems of linguistics, the place and potentialities of the Gaelic genius. . . the synthesis of East and West and the future of civilization. It is a very learned poem involving a stupendous range of reference, especially to Gaelic, Russian, Italian and Indian liter-

atures, German literature and philosophy, and modern physics and the physiology of the brain, and
while mainly in English, utilizes elements of over a
score of languages, Oriental and Occidental.

There is nothing like it in modern literature, nothing even
close. It is an attempt to return poetry to its original role as
repository for all that a culture knows about itself. Unlike
Pound's *Cantos*, it does not merely allude to its extraordinary
range of referents; it explains everything in a persistent, unor-
ganized stream of erudition to match the Joycean stream of
consciousness. Sylvia Townsend Warner described Mac-
Diarmid's autobiography in words that are more applicable to
the poetry: "as though the pages of two encyclopedias were
being turned by a sixty-mile gale." It is a poetry that wants to
raise the standard—both in the sense of hoisting a battle flag
and of educating the world through unremitting instruction
and admonition—and it is a poetry that, uniquely, keeps
reminding us what it ought to be: "The Kind of Poetry I
Want."

Certain poems easily detach themselves—among them,
the earlier "On a Raised Beach," "In the Slums of Glasgow,"
"The Glass of Pure Water," "Direadh III," "Diamond Body,"
and "Once in a Cornish Garden"—and can stand with the
poems of the great 20th-century poets from the Celtic Isles:
Yeats, Basil Bunting, D.H. Lawrence, David Jones. But to
excerpt—as editors of various editions of *Selected Poems* have
been forced to do—from the poems of *Cornish Heroic Song* is to
destroy the effect of MacDiarmid's greatly underestimated
music. Based on Scottish piping and Indian ragas, it is dependent on the counterpoint (MacDiarmid would say dialectic)
between a continuous drone and bursts of melody. The plea-
sures of MacDiarmid are precisely the explosions of passion,
rage, intellectual insight, aphorism, and spiritual transcendence that occur after pages of foreign word-lists and arcane
bibliographies, catalogues of scientific terms and theories, histories of literature and art and philosophy and music, piling
up, as he wrote, like Zouave acrobats. These are the volcanic
fireworks amidst the tons of dead ash; out of context there is

no contrast, and their power is diminished. Rather like excerpting the magnificent landscapes from the *Cantos*, they are the jewels without the crown.

He is one the great materialist poets and one of the great mystics; a poet thoroughly immersed in the technicalities of geology, astronomy, and physics who could also write "The astronomical universe is *not* all there is" and "everything I write, of course,/ Is an extended metaphor for something I never mention." He was a political animal who believed that the role of the poet is to be a solitary contemplative; a man whose millions of words revolve around a center of absolute stillness: "The word with which silence speaks/ Its own silence without breaking it." A Nietzschean Marxist, he thought that the collective, with all its contradictions, could be embodied by one superior man. A Communist from the working class (unlike his English poet contemporaries), he had no pity for the poor, but honored them for their stoicism and loathed them for their ignorance and spiritual decay, "innumerable meat without minds." He expressed his love, in "Once in a Cornish Garden," one of the great love poems, through an astonishingly detailed celebration of his wife's clothes and cosmetics. He wrote in a style that owed nothing to the modern writers he most admired: Joyce, Pound, Rilke, Brecht, Mayakovsky, Hikmet. He may be the only poet of the century for whom, in the poem, philosophy matters. Science was his mythology.

He believed that the first civilization was Ur-Gaelic, and that it arose in Georgia, birthplace of Stalin. He started a Hugh MacDiarmid Book Club, which offered subscribers a new MacDiarmid book every two months. He envisioned a Celtic Union of Socialist Soviet Republics (Scotland, Wales, Ireland, Cornwall) which would join in an "East-West Synthesis" with the Soviet Union. He listed his hobby in *Who's Who* as "Anglophobia." He believed that Cornwall was an outpost of Atlantis. He rejoined the Party after the invasion of Hungary, while simultaneously signing a public letter denouncing it. He believed that "there lie hidden in language elements that, effectively combined, can utterly change the nature of man." He read his poems under huge portraits of Blake and

Whitman in Peking in 1957. He debated on the same side as
Malcolm X at the Oxford Union in defense of extremism. He
said that "Of all the men I have known, I loved Ezra Pound,"
but they only briefly corresponded, and had met only once, in
1970, when Pound had already stopped speaking and
MacDiarmid was nearly deaf. In his eighties he was writing
television reviews. The words he wanted on his tombstone
were "A disgrace to the community," but at his death this was
ignored.

[1993]

CAN I GET A WITNESS?

Though the story is scarcely believable, the example is apt: An early explorer reported that an African tribe had only one song that had only one line: "The King has all the power." Whether this was all the community had to express or all that they were allowed to express, the message is the same: Political poetry is as old and as varied as poetry itself, and as intrinsic to poetry as fertility, love, and death.

For most of this century, the image of political poetry was restricted to that which was plainly written to further a specific movement or goal (revolution, collective liberation, peace). Then, as the ideologies unraveled, academic theory began insisting on an amorphous "political" reading of everything: the silences implicit in the poem about a daffodil. Like much of what is called "theory," it was both perfectly true and a self-evident generality that was all too easy to reiterate in complex ways.

Lately, a new subgenre has been invented to stand for the whole in this ideological interregnum: the poetry of "witness." Anti-New Critical with a vengeance, witness poetry is entirely dependent on biographical background, and is ultra-empirical in a way perhaps unprecedented in literary history. It is a poetry where you had to have been there.

The Qur'an of the witness subgenre is Carolyn Forché's popular anthology, *Against Forgetting*. Limited to the 20th century, poets in the book qualify as witnesses if they have been combatants or civilians in a war, prisoners or exiles, or citizens of a totalitarian regime (regardless of one's life under that regime). More dubiously, also included are journalists or visitors in a war zone, even for a short period, and non-white residents of the United States. (White people, presumably, do not witness injustice in this country.) Others, including those whose poetry is normally considered "political" by any other standards—Allen Ginsberg, for one—might as well have spent their time composing pantoums at the club.

This taxonomy, like the Hindu caste system or editorial policy anywhere, has subtleties of distinction that are impossible for outsiders to grasp. Tadeusz Borowski is a witness of the Holocaust because he was interned in Auschwitz and Dachau. Nelly Sachs is a witness of the Holocaust because she wrote poems about the Holocaust from her exile in Sweden. Irena Klepfitz is a witness of the Holocaust because she was born in Warsaw in 1941 and was hidden in the countryside, emigrated to the United States as a small child, and wrote poems about the Holocaust in New York City. Charles Reznikoff, however, is not a witness of the Holocaust because he was born in the United States and wrote poems about the Holocaust in New York City.

Such literalness and hair-splitting historicism is, incredibly for a poet, a surprisingly absolute denial of imagination. (One hardly demands similar evidence from other writers: snapshots of Laura or Beatrice, or of the poet holding his shoes on Dover Beach.) The "poetry of witness," as a concept—not the poets themselves, but the box they have now been put into—has become a branch of the poetry as autotherapy that is currently being promoted on public broadcasting television and in countless writing schools. A poetry where one's autobiography is primary, incidents of victimization are the salient features of one's life, and writing is seen as the way to heal those psychic wounds. (This last feature is the best evidence that this has nothing to do with poetry at all. Poetry does not close wounds or answer questions; it opens them.) *Against Forgetting*, with its organizing principle of biographical "extremity," is not all that different from a book published a few years ago in Spain, a fat international and historical volume with an ominous black-on-black cover: *The Anthology of Poets Who Committed Suicide*. Once upon a time, it was enough for poets to think, dream, and write, and their first-person was usually a persona. Now they must submit a résumé to be validated for sincerity.

The inherent value of "witnessing" as a measure of poetry is evident in two recent publications. The first is *Outcry from the Volcano*, edited and translated by Jiro Nakano, an anthology of tanka written by Hiroshima survivors, mainly amateur poets, in the years immediately following the devastation. It is both a moving document and of practically no interest as poetry. (And one reads it with amazement: Did not one of these poets feel that the tanka's five lines and counted syllables were somehow inadequate to their experience?) The second is the poems of Araki Yasusada, a postal clerk whose family was erased by the bomb, but who lived on to 1972. His strange and wonderful notebooks were discovered years after his death; lately they have been appearing in translation in *Conjunctions*, *Grand Street*, and other magazines, where they have provoked considerable interest.

The problem is that Yasusada is the pseudonym of an anonymous, possibly American poet, who has brilliantly written all the work, complete with slightly awkward bits of translationese. A telling case: Had rumors of Yasusada's identity not begun to circulate, he would have become "our" primary poet-witness of nuclear disaster—much as the greatest witnessing of plague is Daniel Defoe's entirely fictional first-person account.

Witness poetry, a sign of the times, reduces, yet again, the political to the personal, and confines the act of writing to a factual narcissism. It should be remembered that legal witnesses are not automatically presumed to be reliable. Poets are no more or less credible, regardless of the greatness of the work. Speaking of Hiroshima, here is one of the masters, William Carlos Williams, in a letter to another poet, Byron Vazakas, dated August 7, 1945: "The day following the atomic blast!—the poor Jews who accomplished it. Now we'll hate them worse than ever." And here is another master, Lorine Niedecker, three months later:

> New!
> Reason explodes. Atomic split
> shows one element
> Jew

Postscript: I Found a Witness

The preceding was published in the *Village Voice Literary Supplement* in July 1996 and was the first public declaration of the pseudonymity of Araki Yasusada. A few weeks later, the

American Poetry Review published an issue with a special supplement featuring Yasusada. *APR*, whose trademark is photos
of the poets often larger than the poems themselves, represented the witness poet with what appeared to be the blurred
xerox of a xerox of a xerox of a mug shot of some low-level
yakuza.

The coincidence led to an article in *Lingua Franca*, a gossip
magazine for academics, in which an *APR* editor called the
poems a "criminal act," a proof that they publish poets, not
poems. This, in turn, led to one of those momentary media
frenzies that now routinely accompany any novelty: articles in
the *Wall Street Journal*, the *Manchester Guardian*, the *Sydney
Morning Herald*, and the *Financial Times* of London; a front-
page story in the *Asahi Shimbun*, Japan's largest newspaper; a
conference in Utrecht; symposia in the *Boston Review*, the
Denver Quarterly, *Strand* in England, and in various places on
the Internet—all before the poems were published in book
form.

The first order of speculation was, of course, whodunit. A
poet I vaguely know called me out of the blue—he had never
called before—to ask point-blank if I was Yasusada; he had a
long list of entirely persuasive reasons. An editor at one of the
magazines that had published the poems thought it was her
old boyfriend. Various names were raised and debated, with
the likeliest suspects being the primary purveyors of the
Yasusada manuscripts: Javier Alvarez, a prominent Mexican
composer living in London, and Kent Johnson, an instructor
at a community college in Illinois and the editor of anthologies of American Buddhist and contemporary Russian poetry.

In response to the journalists, Alvarez and Johnson said
the poems were the work of one Tosa Motokiyu, who had
been their roommate in Milwaukee in the 1970's. "Motokiyu"
was, almost needless to say, also a pseudonym, and the person attached to that name had recently died; Alvarez wrote a
moving account of his last hours.

Meanwhile, in a further complication, the Russian critic
Mikhail Epstein rather brilliantly demonstrated that Yasusada
could be the work of either of two well-known Russian writers,
Andrei Bitov and Dmitri Prigov, or a collaboration between

them. Both had previously invented authors—one of them Chinese, another Polish-Italian-Japanese—and both had long-announced, mysteriously unpublished "Japanese" projects. Moreover, in true conspiratologist fashion, Epstein located both writers at a conference in St. Petersburg with none other than Kent Johnson.

In the proliferating discussions, the identity of the author had become so refracted that it approached the condition of We Are All Yasusada. Perhaps it is best to call him/her/them the Yasusada Author, much as we refer to a Renaissance painter as the Master of the X Altar.

The Yasusada debate rather predictably fell into the categories of politics, literary politics, and theory. The political reading was based on the assumption that the author was a white American male, and thus the poems were a cruel, racist, imperialist joke. This was based on the (racist and imperialist) assumption that anyone who is not a white Euromale wants to speak only in an "authentic" voice. It was inconceivable that the Yasusada Author could be a young woman in Chiapas. (In the beginning of the century, there was a Japanese memoirist and novelist, Onoto Watanna, who was a best-selling writer in the West; she turned out to be a half-Chinese Eurasian who lived in Hong Kong.)

In the political debate, Edward Said's *Orientalism* was inevitably cited, much as medieval discussions always deferred to the authority of Isidore of Seville. But, as Said himself says in passing, his dissection of the Orientalism of the "Near" and "Middle" East (those geographical dislocations) becomes less applicable as one goes further East. Western scholars, poets, and philosophers never idealized Arab civilization as the Source of Wisdom in the way that the Enlightenment imagined China or Romanticism India. When one reaches 20th-century Japan, a First World imperialist nation, Said's book hardly applies at all. The Yasusada Author, even if a white American male, is no more an agent of colonialism than a Japanese country & western singer.

The literary-political response centered on two points, both true. One was the current cult of celebrity that has expanded to engulf literature: We now like to have authors attached to books, preferably attractive people or ones with sad lives (or best of all, both). The other was the general ignorance and lack of interest in nearly all foreign poetry. Thus, it was only Yasusada's tragic life, not his poetry, that got him published in leading magazines. And if the poetry seemed radical, it was only because few were familiar with 20th-century Japanese poetry. (In fact, for a far more complex reaction to the war, see Takamura Kōtarō's *A Brief History of Imbecility*.)

Finally, the theory-minded raised the banners of those other Isidores of Seville, Foucault and Barthes, to connect Yasusada to "the death of the author," an advertising campaign that was wildly successful in the academic market, but had limited appeal to readers and writers. It was true that the Yasusada Author refused to step from behind the curtain—at the opposite extreme from Joyce Carol Oates, who writes "pseudonymous" books that are labeled, on the cover, "Joyce Carol Oates writing under the name of . . ."—but pseudonymous authorship, even when fractured into heteronyms (Pessoa) still assigns production to a single named source. True invisibility—the "text itself"—could easily be achieved by publishing every book and every magazine contribution under a different name. Writers, as far as one knows, have never practiced it; if one were that egoless, one wouldn't be a writer.

Yasusada had appeared at a moment when the Eng. Dept. had split into two contradictory "postmodernisms": multiculturalism and deconstruction (and its spin-offs). One side wanted to hear the stories that hadn't been told, and the other doubted that stories could be told; one side promoted authenticity, and the other inauthenticity. The former embraced Yasusada and then violently rejected him when his identity became questionable—the precise moment when the latter embraced him.

Finally, for all the talk of Orientalism and "Japonoiserie," no one has discussed Yasusada as the latest chapter in the American invention of Japanese poetry. The Yasusada poems are very much written in the style, not of Japanese poetry, but of American translations of Japanese poetry, including some

CAN I GET A WITNESS?

witty intentional infelicities and bits of translationese. Moreover, they could only have been written in recent years, for they owe a great deal to the work of Hiroaki Sato.

Sato, the most prolific contemporary translator of classical and modern Japanese poetry has, since the 1970's, vigorously promoted the idea of translating haiku and tanka (and by extension, renga) as single English sentences without line breaks—the way the poems are written out in Japanese. Sato's work has been widely and unjustly reviled by the academics, but it is precisely Sato's form of presentation—not necessarily the Japanese poems themselves—that were clearly determining for the Yasusada Author. (Some have mistakenly attributed the Yasusada prose-poem line to Ron Silliman's so-called "new sentence," which is comparable but not the origin.)

Yasusada, regardless of authorship, is very much an American Japanese poet: a product of the specifically American tradition of translating Japanese poetry. (It is stylistically highly unlikely that the Author is Russian or Spanish or French.) While it is true that the initial reception was due largely to the biography—and in that sense the work was exploitative of the publishing climate and the poems a "hoax"—the creation of the work is clearly an act of empathy and compassion. The Yasusada Author has merely taken the invention of a first-person narrator of a novel one step further: along with speaking, thinking, seeing, feeling, this fictional character now writes. In many ways, the work is far more interesting, full of brilliant details, after one knows that Yasusada is an invention. He is both the greatest poet of Hiroshima and its most unreliable witness.

[1997]

JAMES LAUGHLIN

(1914–1997)

Every consideration of James Laughlin must begin with his List: a list that is numbing to recite, overwhelming in its whole, and astonishing in its particulars. He was the publisher—and almost always the first publisher in the United States—of Apollinaire, Djuna Barnes, Bobrowski, Borges, Paul Bowles, Brecht, Camus, Cela, Céline, Cendrars, Char, Cocteau, Dahlberg, Daumal, Durrell, Eluard, Endo, García Lorca, Hawkes, Hesse, Huidobro, Isherwood, Jarry, Joyce, Kafka, Lautréamont, Merton, Michaux, Henry Miller, Mishima, Montale, Nabokov, Neruda, Parra, Pasternak, Paz, Queneau, Raja Rao, Reverdy, Rilke, Sartre, Supervielle, Svevo, Dylan Thomas, Ungaretti, Valéry, Vittorini, Nathanael West, and Tennessee Williams (to mention only the dead). At a time when they were half-forgotten—it seems incredible now—he brought back into print Henry James, F. Scott Fitzgerald, Evelyn Waugh, E.M. Forster, William Faulkner. For decades he had the only editions of Baudelaire and Rimbaud. And his press, New Directions, was, and continues to be, the Central Station for English-language avant-gardist poetry: Pound, Williams, H.D., Rexroth, Patchen, Oppen, Reznikoff, Olson, Duncan, Creeley, Snyder, Levertov, Bronk, McClure, Braithwaite, Rothenberg, Antin, Sobin, Palmer, Gander, Rosmarie Waldrop, Susan Howe, and so many others. Laughlin was more than the greatest American publisher of the 20th century; his press *was* the 20th century.

Every writer has a tale of conversion—"the book that made me want to become a writer"—and for nearly every writer I know, that one book was published by Laughlin: *Amerika, Nausea, Nightwood, A Season in Hell*, among them, or even *A Coney Island of the Mind*. [Mine was Paz's *Sun Stone*, in the Rukeyser translation.] I belong to the last generation to come of age before the tidal wave of the overproduction of everything, and in my adolescence, the black-and-white photographic covers of ND books were unmistakable on the

bookstore shelves. I would buy any of them at random, knowing that if Laughlin published it, it was something that had to
be read, the latest oracle from the Temple of the Modern, the
place where one went to feel alive in the present.

Laughlin's success is usually attributed to his wealth,
which is only part of the story. He was, of course, an heir to a
steel fortune: the huge sign of Jones & Laughlin used to dom-
inate the cliffs of Pittsburgh. In an interview a few years ago,
he casually mentioned that on the day he graduated Harvard
in 1936, his father gave him $100,000 to start out in the world.
[Context: my parents, a few years older than Laughlin, tell me
that in 1936 their middle-class jobs in New York City together
were earning $2,000 a year.] The young Laughlin was tall,
handsome, athletic, and extremely rich, and could easily have
become a playboy. In fact, he did become a playboy, but a
playboy devoted to literature.

One must understand the milieu from which Laughlin
came: the steel barons of Pittsburgh; the Mellons, Carnegies,
Fricks. Scottish Presbyterians, they counted every penny as
they spent millions. Their philosophy was articulated in a book
by Andrew Carnegie with a priceless title, *The Gospel of Wealth,*
and it was a combination of paternalism and charity. Wealth
was not for personal enjoyment, but was to be held "in trust"
and dispensed according to the wisdom of the man intelligent
enough to have earned it. This meant, on the one hand, that the
Mellons, Carnegies, and Fricks were lavish in endowing the
universities, foundations, museums, symphony halls, and hospitals that still bear their names. On the other hand, they could
be ruthless when their metaphorical children became unruly,
quite openly arranging for the repression of strikers and the
assassinations of union leaders in the steel mills.

Although Laughlin, as far as one knows, never paid for
the murder of anyone—even book reviewers—he did dedi-
cate his fortune to good works. Only a few other wealthy heirs
have been involved in publishing ventures, all of which were
either short-lived or quickly turned into commercial enter-
prises. Money is usually wasted on the rich.

Laughlin not only devoted his life to the unglamourous
pursuit of making books, he also, almost uniquely, did not

name his press after himself. His only sign of self-monumen-
talization was a small line that appeared on the copyright
page of every book, with a strange preposition: "New
Directions books are published for James Laughlin." Not *by*:
for. It was a tip of the hat to the legacy of Andrew Carnegie.

His wealth could have led to a long list of mediocrities. That
it did not was due not only to his evident literary acumen, but
to his modernist commitment to the "new," his knowledge—
now extinct among American editors—of various European
languages, and his willingness to listen to writers (not critics,
reviewers, agents, and makers of buzz) in the search for new
writers. Laughlin's life is a tangle of paths: His prep school
classics teacher, Dudley Fitts, put him in touch with Pound,
who led him to William Carlos Williams, who led him to
Nathanael West. Pound led to Henry Miller who led to
Hesse's *Siddhartha*, the blockbuster that supported dozens of
obscure poets. Williams led to Rexroth who led to Snyder who
led to Bei Dao; Dame Sitwell to Dylan Thomas; Eliot to Djuna
Barnes; Tennessee Williams to Paul Bowles.

     Moreover, he was a fundamentalist believer in the
Poundian idea of "tradition." This was not the canon as
taught in the fossilized universities before the age of "rele-
vance," but a rediscovery, rereading, and reinvention of all
Western and Eastern literatures. The idea—now erased by
postmodernism, and almost quaint—was that the classics
should be read by every intelligent person, that to *be* intelligent one had to read the classics.

     What would be built on this bedrock of the Old (or more
exactly, a new Old) were the new classics: the "good literature" which Laughlin so often said he was publishing. These
were more than good books—not so long ago, all publishers
thought they were publishing at least some good books. These
were the books that would endure, the new books that were
as essential to one's education as the old, the books that you,
reader, ought to be reading.

     The introductions Laughlin wrote for the early New
Directions anthologies are flags waving from the barricades.
But unlike other revolutionaries, he was not disillusioned by

the lack of immediate results. Following Pound, he believed that it takes at least twenty years for a writer to be recognized. (Today it is either twenty minutes or half a century.) So while other publishers treated their titles like fresh fish, Laughlin was the only one to keep almost all his books in print for decades. It was another legacy of 19th-century capitalism, now forgotten—the idea of the long-term investment—and it eventually paid off. Yesterday's bizarre gibberish is now on the final exam.

Ezra Pound told the 20-year-old James Laughlin that he would never be a poet and that he should do something useful, like publishing. Pound—who usually was remarkably skillful in discovering young writers—was so wrong in this case that one suspects him of acting out of self-interest. Laughlin continued to write, but for most of his life he kept it a half-hidden secret. Only in recent years did he begin to regularly publish what turned into a small mountain of poems, essays, memoirs, and fiction.

In his poetry, he evolved an unadorned and direct speech learned from Greek and Latin and from Williams and Rexroth. He invented the only new prosodic form in American poetry since Williams' three-stepped line: each line, composed on the typewriter, cannot be more than one letter-space longer or shorter than the previous line. It was a crackpot idea that worked. Along with Rexroth, he was the author of long, narrative, autobiographical poems that remain pure poetry while being as readable as prose. And he wrote, following his Greek, Latin, and Sanskrit masters, perhaps the only witty erotic American poetry in this century. (It is a curiosity of American poetry that its greatest heterosexual erotic poetry has tended to be written by men and women in their old age.) Now that the poets can no longer demand that Laughlin read them, perhaps they will begin to read him.

His prose style is a strange and highly entertaining combination of an erudite speaking in plain American, a Joycean addicted to puns, and the kind of language one hears in the screwball comedies of the 1930's—the slang of fast-talking eccentrics in tuxedos. There is nothing like his critical writings, especially now, when literary critics employ a language more suited to that of astrophysicists.

James Laughlin was the last American veteran of the revolution of the word, the last with personal memories of all the masters of modernism. He changed Gertrude Stein's flat tire, identified Dylan Thomas' body in the morgue, shipped ballet shoes to Céline's wife after the war, was saved from falling off a cliff by Nabokov's butterfly net, paid for Delmore Schwartz's shrink and Pound's legal defense, smuggled Merton out of the monastery to go drinking, went on mule trips with Rexroth, took tea with Eliot.

He lived from the First World War to the First World Web, the eighty monstrous years on the planet in which all younger writers wish they had lived. He had the self-deprecation of the unusually tall; he would disappear for months to go skiing at Alta, the resort he founded; he was obsessed with döppelgangers, though few mortals were his size; his mannerisms were oddly reminiscent of George Bush; his personal library was unparalleled, and he had read it all; he used to golf with James J. Angleton; he had a passion for India; he was an athlete and a hypochondriac; he sent Clinton—whom he called "Smiley"—a copy of Pound's *ABC of Economics* as an inaugural gift; he was self-absorbed and generous, hedonistic and depressive, obstinate and remarkably receptive; those he published and those he didn't never stopped complaining about him; sheep grazed on his lawn in Connecticut.

[1997]

OMAR CÁCERES

All the stories from the capitals have grown familiar, but where are the histories and accounts of modernism as it was lived and practiced in the provinces? Latin America, for example, in the first half of the century, has shelves of unwritten magical realist literary biographies: The Peruvian Martín Adán, whose first book made him famous at twenty, and who then checked himself into an insane asylum, where he lived for another sixty years, writing on scraps of paper he threw away that were dutifully collected by the orderlies and sent to his publisher. Jorge Cuesta, a poet and the leading Mexican critic of the 1930's, who castrated and slowly fatally poisoned himself as part of his alchemical experiments. Carlos Oquendo de Amat, a Lima street kid who published one book, *5 Meters of Poems*, on a folded sheet of paper five meters long, then gave up writing to join the Communist Party, and knocked in and out of jails and tuberculosis wards in a half-dozen countries before dying in Spain just before the Civil War. Joaquin Pasos, a Nicaraguan who also died young, who wrote *Poems of a Young Man Who Has Never Traveled*, which are all about foreign places; *Poems of a Young Man Who Has Never Been in Love*, which are all love poems; and *Poems of a Young Man Who Doesn't Speak English*, which are written in English. Isaac Berliner, who ran a shop that sold figurines of the saints in a backwater Mexican town, and wrote poems in Yiddish about oppressed peasants that were illustrated by Diego Rivera. Felisberto Hernández, a writer of stories unlike any others, who lived with his mother and wrote in a windowless basement, who paid for the publication of his books by playing the piano in bars in the Uruguayan hinterland, and who died so fat the funeral home had to remove a window to get the coffin out.

And Omar Cáceres: A Chilean, born in 1906, who worked as a violinist in an all-blind orchestra, of which he was the only sighted member. In 1933, hearing that a group of young poets was meeting in a café to put together an anthology of

117

the new Chilean poetry, he walked in, waited until one of them was alone, gave him a poem, and left. The group wrote him, asking for more work, and he agreed to meet on a busy street corner. He handed over a manuscript and kept walking—a tall, thin figure with empty eyes and the "elegance of a ghost," as one of the poets, decades later, recalled. In 1934, his brother paid for the publication of a book of fifteen poems, *Defense of the Idol* (*Defensa del ídolo*). The book, somehow, had an introduction by Vicente Huidobro, the only one he ever wrote for another poet, though it is unlikely the two met. (Could it be a forgery?) Cáceres, disturbed by some typographical errors in the book, burned all the copies he could find. Only two are known to survive. In 1943, the exact date is unknown, he was murdered by assailants unknown for reasons unknown. All that remains of his work are those fifteen poems and a statement, "I, Old and New Words," that he wrote for the anthology. ("Those who have loved greatly and have contemplated the WHY of their suffering when they lost forever what they loved, those are the ones that must understand me.") Nothing else was published elsewhere, and nothing else is known about him.

Here is a translation of the first poem in the book, a hint of how truly weird these poems are, with their continual shifts of register, ironic (or possibly not ironic) bits of inflated language, mysterious references, unlikely word-choices, torments of taboo, and sudden outbursts of confession:

Mansion of Foam

With my heart, beating you, o unbounded shadow,
I graze the total zest of these eternal-images;
he who flees, escaping his life, I think, cleanses the world,
and so is allowed to reflect his sweetly earthly likeness.

A village (Blue), laboriously flooded.
The hard season will come balancing its landscapes.
Time fallen from the trees, whatever sky could be my sky.
The white road crosses its motionless storm.

Speechless voice that lives under my dreams,
my friend instructs me in the naked accent of her arms,
beside the balcony of disciplined light tumultuous,
from where one is warned of still-undreamed misfortune.

Dressed again in distance, between man and
        meager-man,
everything is wrecked "under the banner of the
        final adieu";
I gave up existing, I soon fell abandoned by myself,
for a man loves only his own, obscure life.

Unknown idol. What must I do to give it a kiss?
Legislator of urban time, unfolded, rushing, copious,
I confess my crime against myself because I want to
        understand it,
and on the reefs of its rock alcohol I spread out
        my words.

If he hadn't died before my birth, I would be convinced that I
had met Cáceres. At sixteen, for no particular reason, I was
hitchhiking and jumping freight trains in the Atacama desert
in the north of Chile, staying at mining camps where the
workers, astonished and amused by this sudden apparition of
a gringo naif, would feed me and let me sleep in the barracks.
One of the camps was a sulfur mine at 18,000 feet, where I
could barely walk or breathe or see from the clouds of sulfur
dust, and where the miners survived with wads of coca leaves
and lime in their cheeks. A week after I left, the whole camp
was buried in a landslide.

The only hostility I met was at a huge copper strip mine,
the largest in the world, owned and run by Americans. I was
not a novelty for the Texan bosses, just a crazy kid, and they
threw me out as soon as I arrived. I spent the night hungry
and unsleeping on a slag heap.

The next morning, the first truck that finally came by
picked me up. Having told the driver I was a poet, he recited
Pablo Neruda to me, and then asked me to sing my poems.
Humiliated, I could only mollify him with a few scraps of

García Lorca. Hours later we came to a large town, and I asked to be let off. "Are you sure?" "Sure." He smiled and drove off.

I had wandered for a few blocks, wondering at the ornate but faded facades and signs, before I realized that there was no one there. I walked on, panicked. The town, like all the towns in that desert, was dust-blown and forlorn, but none of the buildings, far grander than elsewhere, was in ruins. The town was entirely intact, and empty.

Then, some blocks away, I saw a figure walking toward me through the knee-high clouds of dust. Not a ghost, but a gaunt middle-aged man in a three-piece black suit, shiny in places and dirt-caked in others, with a starched, formerly white shirt and a stick-pinned black tie, and he greeted me without surprise.

The town had mined bauxite and boomed at the turn of the century, until the invention of an artificial substitute had caused its collapse. He took me through the bank buildings, the Grand Hotel, the telegraph office, the enormous opera house where Jenny Lind and the other stars of Joseph Cornell boxes had once sang. Some company still owned the town, and he had been hired to look after it. He lived alone with his ancient, shriveled, shawled, and completely silent mother.

The three of us ate a silent lunch of chicken broth and rice with bottles of unlabeled wine. Then he walked me out to the main road, gravely and ceremoniously shook my hand, and vanished. I waited many hours for the first truck to come and, with time, forgot him until I read *Defense of the Idol*.

[1997]

WHAT WAS FORMALISM?

I have recently come across an anthology with a fire-alarm red cover, an inflammatory title (*Rebel Angels*) above a reproduction of Blake's flaming exemplar, and a gaseous introduction whose first word is "Revolution." It is not, as one might expect, a lost artifact of the Beat Generation, but rather a Molotov cocktail tossed by the radical right of poetry, the self-styled "New Formalists."

According to these Rebel Angels—who, like most conservatives, have short historical memories for what they are conserving—it was during the "cultural upheavals of the 60's and 70's," not fifty or sixty years before, that formalism, defined as "meter and rhyme," was "largely . . . abandoned by American poets." The result was that "poetry and prose became nearly indistinguishable" (leading, no doubt, to the popularity of projective verse mysteries at the beach). Happily, however, certain poets—Wilbur, Nemerov, Hecht, Van Duyn, among them—"courageous in their commitment to their art," withstood the onslaught, kept the faith, and inspired a renaissance launched by those misfits from the Generation of '68 for whom *baba* was a rhyme-scheme and not a guru, and who are now in their forties and fifties.

The formalism they have collectively revived is not merely "the art of making poems in measured speech." It "assumes a valued civility. . . a larger cultural vision that restores harmony and balance to the arts." According to the poet Timothy Steele, formalist poetry, more than any "other pursuit," can "nourish"

> a love of nature, an enthusiasm for justice, a readiness of good humor, a spontaneous susceptibility to beauty and joy, an interest in our past, a hope for our future, and, above all, a desire that others should have the opportunity and encouragement to share these qualities

which presumably were and are absent from "free verse," not to mention the "other" pursuits. The thought that justice and equal opportunity are the hallmarks of a flourishing formalist verse culture (such as Victorian England, the Court of Versailles, Heian Kyoto . . .) belongs in a parallel universe, perhaps one where a group named after Lucifer & Co. promotes hope, good humor, beauty, and joy.

Rebel Angels collects the poems, each labeled with the form it employs, of twenty-five poets "deserving attention for the beauty, accuracy and memorability of their language, as well as their feelings and ideas." They "represent nothing less than a revolution, a fundamental change, in the art of poetry as it is practiced in this country"—and, if poets deserve attention for their feelings, a revolution in criticism as well.

As a devotee of poetic revolutions, formal or informal, I cracked the book at random, hoping for a new specter haunting America. These were the first lines of the first poem I read:

> We stood on the rented patio
> While the party went on inside.
> You knew the groom from college.
> I was a friend of the bride.

Every revolution must suffer a few setbacks, so I flipped again, to a rebel sonnet:

> Four years ago I started reading Proust.
> Although I'm past the halfway point, I still
> Have seven hundred pages of reduced
> Type left before I reach the end. I will . . .

Charles Reznikoff used to say, "When I come to a poem like this, I turn the page." On to another sonnet, titled, unpromisingly, "The View from an Airplane at Night, Over California":

> This is a sight that Wordsworth never knew . . .

Quite true, but I'd thought that this particular trope had been buried forever by Kenneth Koch, forty years ago, in his

famous parody of academic verse: "This Connecticut landscape would have pleased Vermeer. . . ."

Turning the pages, there were too many titles and open-
ing lines that inspired me to turn the page: "On Leaving the
Artist's Colony"; "Convalescing in London"; "Remembering
the Ardèche"; "Grand Central Station, 20 December 1987"
("The clock's so huge you can watch the minute hand"); "Back
Trouble" ("And so to bed . . ."); "Approaching a Significant
Birthday, He Peruses *The Norton Anthology of Poetry*";
"Moments of Summer"; an unironic "To Be Sung on the
Fourth of July"; "Blue Jay" ("A sound like a rusty pump
beneath our window/ Woke us at dawn. Drawing the curtains back,/ We saw—through milky light, above the dog-
house—/ A blue jay lecturing a neighbor's cat."); "Dinner at
Le Caprice"; "Those Paperweights with Snow Inside" (speaking of "accuracy," they're called snow globes); and so on
through bland but happy career lives, now apparently available to poets, male and female, of all races, regions, and sexual preferences (all of which are represented here). The only
note of incivility was a leering sexuality ("The Rapist's
Villanelle," "Satyr, Cunnilinguent: To Herman Melville,"
"Victoria's Secret") that was creepy in its adolescent *frisson* of
formalism and pseudo-lewdness, and entirely lacking in genuine perversity—as is found in that bizarre form-meister,
Philip Larkin, who used to exchange spanking magazines
with the expert on Stalin's atrocities.

But I paused at a numbing title, "The Lost Bee," because
the line by Allen Tate which inspired the poem—"As a lost
bee returning to the hive"—seemed to embody an eighth type
of ambiguity, lack of sense. (As Mark Twain said, "I wasn't
lost, just slightly misplaced.") "The Lost Bee" begins:

> When I returned to the hive I was one
> Among many, in a blistering hum.
> A braid of air had brought me far from home
> —Blinder than flowers, simpler than the sun . . .

The poem, involving some sort of first-person apian epiphany,
was as bad as "braid of air" promises, but what interested me

was its identification, in the forms index, as "envelope quatrains, iambic tetrameter, iambic pentameter." An envelope quatrain rhymes, like the elegists of the Dancing Queen, *abba*, as the first quatrain did (with a slight "slant" on hum/home). The second quatrain had further slight slants: curves/serve and give/grave. But the third and then the fourth increasingly slanted off the rhyme charts: god/strand, lose/skies, dance/space, and sense/encodes. This was starting to look like that dreaded tennis without a net, free verse itself. (If "encodes" rhymes with "sense," so does any other word in the language ending with an "s" sound.) Then I went back to the first quatrain, quoted above. The second line had only managed one iamb in its four feet—in athletics it would have been a disqualification. On the next page was a poem by the same author labeled as "alternating, envelope, and ballad quatrains, iambic trimeter." Five of the ten quatrains were none of these forms, and a stanza like "And the brightest halo/ Shrinks to a shadow/ Gray as a noose./ Intangible truths" was hardly iambic or trimetric.

I began to suspect that the vaunted strictures of the New Formalism were rather like the rules in a household with small children: tiny attempts at maintaining order, frequently reiterated, and rarely observed. Very few Rebel Angels attempted anything more difficult than a sonnet, and only a few even tried their civil hands at these. Many of the poems merely kept to regular stanza forms, without rhyme—as countless "free verse" poems do. The rhymes themselves were astonishingly banal (brook/book, well/tell, park/dark, eye/sky, storm/warm, etc); not a one even approached the wit of popular song: Bob Dylan ("the pump don't work/ 'cause the vandals/took the handles") or Smokey Robinson or Moss Hart or Curtis Mayfield or John Lennon or anything by Cole Porter ("Let's throw away anxiety, let's quite forget propriety,/ Respectable society, the rector and his piety,/ And contemplate l'amour in all its infinite variety,/ My dear, let's talk about love.").

And nearly every poem was written in three, four, or five feet of iambs. What is difficult, as Pound said at the beginning of the century, is *not* to write in iambs: "to break the HEAVE."

After all, most of what we say in English is an unstressed monosyllabic personal pronoun or possessive or preposition or article followed by a stressed monosyllabic noun or verb (one iamb) or a disyllabic noun or verb stressed on its first syllable (one and a half iambs). Most polysyllabic words have alternating stresses. When one adds the permissible trochee at the beginning of the line, the permissible anapests anywhere, and all the other little infractions—exceptions that are supposed to make the rule—it may well be that the iamb is no more a formal quality than standard spelling.

Add to this the facts that the division into strictly stressed and unstressed syllables is inappropriate to English, that a line may have many possible scansions according to how it is read ("Shall I compare thee to a summer's day?"), and that off-rhymes, some quite far-fetched, "count" in a rhyme-scheme, and we are left with a system of measurement as organic and untechnical as Williams' much-derided "variable foot" (which, by the way, is what English-language poets have always practiced). The only American formalists of the century may well turn out to be Louis Zukofsky, John Cage, and Jackson Mac Low, who invented their own, idiosyncratic and inflexible rules: placement of letters according to mathematical or mystical formulae, predetermined word-lists and selection processes, and so on.

I'm sorry, but these Rebel Angels are wimps, café Republicans measuring out their lives in coffee spoons that keep changing size. For real formalism, we must go to the Old Formalism, to the days when forms were forms and form had nothing to do with etiquette. We must go back, that is, to the Vikings:

Viking formalism meant, for example, that to write a mere epitaph of ordinary statements and sentiments for a tomb—such as "Here lies a warrior famed for his virtue. Denmark will never know a more honorable sea captain, or one stronger in battle"—one began with a common stanza form, such as the *dróttkvatt*.

This stanza form had eight lines, broken into two half-stanzas of four lines, each expressing a single thought, that

were, in turn, divided into two couplets. Each line had six syllables; only three could be stressed (and Old Norse, as one can
imagine, had genuine stresses). The first line of each couplet
had to have two stressed syllables that began with the same
sound, which was also the sound of the first stressed syllable
in the next line. (The other stressed syllables could not alliter-
ate.) The two stressed alliterative syllables in the first line
could not rhyme; but the first stressed alliterative syllable in
the second line had to rhyme with another syllable in the
same line to which it was not alliterative.

The word order was completely unlike that of prose. For
example, the structure of a normal prose sentence of 16 words
(taking 1, 2, 3, etc., as the words in their proper prose order)
looks like this in a relatively simple half-stanza:

$$
\begin{array}{llll}
2 & 4 & 5 & 3 \\
1 & 8 & 9 & 6 & 7 \\
12 & 10 & 13 & 14 \\
11 & 15 & 16
\end{array}
$$

In a more complex poem, poetic syntax is further
stretched by fragmenting and reassembling the clauses. For
example, back to the sea captain and the first half-stanza.
("Here lies a warrior famed for his virtue. . .") The poet
employs a *kenning*, or epithet, for warrior ("the one who carried out the work of Þruðr, goddess of battles"), and the whole
sentence reads literally: "Under this mound is hidden the one
who carried out the work of Þruðr, goddess of battles, whom
the greatest virtues accompanied; most men knew that."
(Though the Old Norse only has 15 words.)

The poem (keeping the literal English prose syntax)
breaks this into something like:

Under this mound   whom the greatest
most men knew that   virtues
accompanied   the one who carried out the work of Þruðr
goddess of battles   is hidden

The pattern of clauses is thus:

1a	3a
4	3b
3c	2a
2b	1b

This was merely a tombstone epitaph, not a particularly memorable poem. It was written, as all poetry was, in a single line. (The ragged right-hand margin is a by-product of the availability of cheap paper.) There were no spaces between the words. The form of the poem was musically, not visually, evident—and evident to all its readers or listeners—and was only one of many such forms, most of them even more complex.

In a famous Icelandic story in the sagas, Hallbjörn of Þingvellir wanted to compose a poem in praise of a dead poet. He fell asleep on the poet's burial mound and dreamed that the mound opened and a tall man appeared, who said, "There you lie, Hallbjörn of Þingvellir, trying to do something you are incapable of doing—composing a poem in praise of me." The dead poet then taught Hallbjörn all the forms while he dreamed. They took many years to master, but in the end he wrote his poem.

[1998]

ACKERLEY'S *HINDOO HOLIDAY*

The double-o in the title immediately signals that we are returning to another time; one that was not so long ago, but is now as antiquated as its orthography. An era that was tragic, perhaps, in its essence, but comic in its particulars; a time of unspeakable wealth and inconceivable poverty, continual cultural misunderstandings, unfettered whimsy, and cruelties large and small: the age of the British Raj and the Indian princes.

The Raj was born in the wake of the 1857 Sepoy Revolt against the Honourable East India Company, which had controlled much of the subcontinent for a hundred years. Realizing that the Company could no longer protect British interests, the British government, with some reluctance, intervened. Slightly more than half of the country fell under the direct administration of the Crown, but the rest of the land was divided into 562 states, from tiny principalities to kingdoms large as the British Isles themselves. These states enjoyed varying degrees of autonomy in their internal affairs, but all had to pledge not to pursue independent courses of foreign policy.

This meant peace for hundreds of kingdoms that had spent centuries warring. And it meant that the princes, whose pride was based on a heritage of martial valor, had to find new ways of demonstrating their princeliness. Many found the solution in the overflowing coffers of their treasuries. With war no longer draining their time and revenues, they attacked leisure as though it were the citadel of an ancient rival.

There were palaces with seven thousand servants, and a Maharani whose jewels were so heavy she could only stand when supported by two attendants. There were royal hunts on the backs of four hundred elephants, where scores of tigers or tens of thousands of birds would be slain in a single day. There were children's toys of solid gold, nursery balls encrusted with rubies, a turban with three thousand diamonds, a carpet made only of jewels.

There was a Maharajah who changed his clothes when the thermometer rose or fell by one degree, and one who sent his laundry to Paris. There was an auto enthusiast with 270 cars for his personal motoring, and a Scotophile who outfitted his idle troops in complete Highland gear (with the addition of pink tights, so that the brown knees of his men would take on a ruddy Scots complexion). There was one, unlucky in love, who checked into a Paris hotel, ordered cases of Dom Perignon, and drank until he died. And another who occupied thirty-five suites of the Savoy in London and received three thousand fresh roses a day, for he said he loved nature.

A fantastic spire atop the most hierarchical society in the East, princely India was administered or advised by the stodgy, lower-middle-class members of the military and bureaucratic castes of the most hierarchical society in the West. Transformed by colonialism into aristocrats, these *sahibs* and *memsahibs* inhabited a world of pig-sticking and costume balls, puttees and topees, tinned peas and quinine, calling cards and chits. A world that was ritualized in its slightest details to preserve its newly found decorum in the vastness of an India teeming with germs and masses: a chaos to be largely ignored but strictly controlled when it entered the home or barracks or office in the form of the retinues of servants.

J. R. Ackerley wandered into this scene in 1923. The handsome son of an extravagantly *nouveau riche* fruiterer—the self-styled "Banana King of London"—he had gone directly from his militaristic public school into the trenches soon after war was declared. He saw action at the Somme (where a million and a half shells were fired, and sixty thousand British soldiers killed or wounded on the first day alone) and in other terrible battles; lost his idolized brother; was wounded and taken prisoner; and was not returned to England until months after the peace.

He then entered Cambridge, and a homosexual world that itself now seems as remote as the Raj. Still under the shadow of the Oscar Wilde trial and the Sodomy Laws, more circumspect than closeted, it was a tiny universe of brilliant upper-class men who reveled and suffered under a sharp class distinction between sex and friendship. As detailed in Peter Parker's witty biography of Ackerley, they talked endlessly to each other about their sex lives, but would select their actual partners from the working class. Often heterosexual and sometimes married, their lovers—unlike themselves—had little spare time and little to say that would be of interest to Oxbridge. Romance was furtive, brief, complicated to arrange, thrilling, and boring.

In 1923, Ackerley was twenty-seven, had published a few poems, written a play, *The Prisoners of War*, that was having trouble finding a producer because of its implicit homoeroticism, and was adrift. His friend E. M. Forster suggested a stint in India, from which Forster had recently returned, perhaps as the secretary to the Maharajah of Chhatarpur, a minor prince whom Forster called "the Prince of Muddlers, even among Indian muddlers." The Maharajah was fifty-nine, tiny, slightly crippled, an eccentric dresser, and notoriously ugly, with the collapsed face of a Pekinese; he was also gay.

Months of negotiation followed. The Maharajah had wanted a secretary who was exactly like Olaf, a character in H. Rider Haggard's *The Wanderer's Necklace*, and had even written to Haggard for help. He was oddly unimpressed by Ackerley's photograph, then impressed by his poems, offered him lifetime employment leading to a cabinet post, dismissed the whole thing as impossible, and finally hired him for six months. Ackerley ended up staying less than five. His duties largely consisted of driving around with the Maharajah in one of his many cars; answering—or more exactly, avoiding answering—sudden questions on metaphysics or ethics; ogling boys with the lonely regent and commiserating with his imagined ailments and ill-starred horoscopes; entertaining insufferably dim British guests; writing letters to the Political Agent concerning the construction of a Greek temple where young men could lounge and discuss philosophy; and trying to keep his distance from the inevitable exceedingly minor palace intrigues.

Back in England, Ackerley slowly transformed his Indian diaries into *Hindoo Holiday*, which appeared in 1932. His publisher, fearful of libel, had insisted on cuts in the text pertaining to the Maharajah's sexual preferences and speculations on the paternity of his heirs. Chhatarpur was jokingly changed to Chhokrapur, which means "City of Boys." Nevertheless, it was too salacious to be broadcast on the BBC, and salacious enough to become an instant and unexpected hit. Vita Sackville-West, Evelyn Waugh, and Cyril Connolly loved it. André Gide recommended it to Gallimard, and the Aga Khan, the playboy spiritual leader of the Ismailis, not only insisted on writing a preface to the French edition, but also named a race horse after the book. (Unfortunately it was a loser.) The book remained in print for decades. A new edition in 1952 restored some of the cuts, but it was not, strangely, until its first Indian edition in 1979 that readers could find a completely unexpurgated text.

Ackerley went on to become the much-loved literary editor of *The Listener* from 1935 to 1959, and to write, at tortoise pace, three more books: an extraordinary portrait of his Alsatian, *My Dog Tulip* (1956); an autobiographical novel, *We Think the World of You* (1960), which was rejected by Maurice Girodias as "not nearly dirty enough," but became a scandalous prizewinner; and the frank and pioneering memoir, *My Father and Myself*, which Ackerley had begun in 1933 and finished just before his death in 1967.

V. S. Naipaul, recalling his first visit to India (in *The Enigma of Arrival*) writes:

> India was special to England; for two hundred years there had been any number of English travelers' accounts and, latterly, novels. I could not be that kind of traveler. In traveling to India I was traveling to an un-English fantasy, and a fantasy unknown to Indians of India. . . . There was no model for me here, in this exploration; neither Forster nor Ackerley nor Kipling could help.

It is an indication of the place that *Hindoo Holiday* held on the short shelf of enduring literary books produced by the Raj:

preceded only by Emily Eden's *Up the Country* in the mid-19th century and, of course, by *Kim* and *A Passage to India*. Later it was followed by L. H. Myers' *The Root and the Flower* (also known as *The Near and the Far*, a tetralogy of philosophical novels set in the Mughal age, and thus a product of the Raj but not about it) and Paul Scott's operatic *The Raj Quartet*, with its nostalgic coda, *Staying On*. The literature's final flowering was, appropriately, not written by an Englishman, but by a fiercely Anglophilic Bengali, Nirad C. Chaudhuri, in his half-Proustian, half-polemical *Autobiography of an Unknown Indian*.

Hindoo Holiday is the most comic of these, and the only one to avoid larger issues, eternal mysteries, or the temptation to throng with as much life as India itself. Ackerley was clearly severe in reworking his diaries, limiting himself to the creation of a handful of unforgettable characters, and eliminating anything he experienced outside of Chhatarpur itself. There is no description of his journey to the state, and none of his departure; a three-week trip to Benares and other places is discussed only in terms of the complex negotiations with the Maharajah for a leave; and there is no mention of the famed erotic temples of Khajaraho, which were nearby and which he surely visited. Instead, he essentially transplanted the comedy of manners from an English country house to an Indian palace; this may be the only travel book ever written that could easily be adapted as a play.

Ackerley makes no pretense that this is anything more than a holiday; he does not presume to characterize, let alone condemn, the Indian soul, based on his chance encounters. (And in fact he is often a little fuzzy or simply wrong on Indian details.) Kipling loved India, and especially the words of Anglo-India—the first half of *Kim* has an exuberance of language that would not be seen again until Joyce—but he still bore the white man's burden. Ackerley, even more than Forster, has no agenda; both are extraordinarily tolerant, reserving their scorn—like many travelers—only for their fellow countrymen (who in *Hindoo Holiday* actually speak of the "dark and tortuous minds of the natives").

That this was due to their lives as sexual outsiders is unquestionable. Although it seems unimaginable now—given the prudishness, until quite recently, of modern India, with its covered and secluded women, and where even a kiss was forbidden on a movie screen—it was sexual licentiousness that was at the root of the Raj's horror of the land. The biggest selling book on India before *Hindoo Holiday* was Katherine Mayo's 1927 *Mother India*, which claimed that the "degeneracy" of the Indian race was due not to poverty or the tyrannies of its various rulers, but rather to promiscuity:

> The whole pyramid of Indians' woes, material and spiritual—poverty, sickness, ignorance, political minority, melancholy, ineffectiveness, not forgetting that subconscious conviction of inferiority which he forever bares and advertises by his gnawing and imaginative alertness for social affronts—rests upon a rock-bottom physical base. The base is simply, his manner of getting into the world and his sex-life thenceforward.

Even worse than sex, of course, was interracial sex: It is the enigma around which *A Passage to India* turns, and the revulsion of it propels the violence of *The Raj Quartet*. In contrast, the one kiss in *Hindoo Holiday*— between Ackerley and one of the young men who hang around his bungalow—is merely a funny and sweet moment of no significance. The Maharajah's pursuit of his boy actors is presented as comically as his long drives in search of good omens (turning the car around when something appears on the unlucky left so that it will be on the lucky right) or the hapless tutor Abdul's pursuit of better employment. Ackerley's descriptions of the beauties of the boys he sees are as relaxed and natural as his descriptions of wildlife; they are entirely without the psychodrama or the Hellenistic pretensions that were common among gay writers at the time. This offhand and funny presentation of the potentially shocking would become an Ackerley trademark. *My Father and Myself* famously begins: "I was born in 1896 and my parents were married in 1919."

No English writer had such uncomplicated fun in India; none could create such comic characters without condescension; no one, until Salman Rushdie and the current generation of Indian novelists, could write dialogue in Indian English so well. Above all, *Hindoo Holiday* is as perfectly constructed as *A Passage to India*, though because of its pose as a travel book and not a novel, few seemed to have noticed.

[1999]

SIMILES OF BEAUTY

The handsome youth sees the beautiful maiden seemingly for the first time:

> She had a face like a full moon, and eyes like a blue lotus; she had arms graceful like the stalk of a lotus, and a lovely full bosom; she had a neck marked with three lines like a shell, and magnificent coral lips . . . .

The description is in *The Ocean Made of Streams of Story*, and this being India, it is not the first time that he and she have clapped eyes; they were married in a previous birth. The tireless annotator Penzer notes that "the Hindus always admired the full breast. This was also considered a *sine qua non* among the Samoans. The Arabs insisted on firmness rather than size." And he is reminded of this passage from a similar scene in *The Thousand and One Nights* in the Burton translation:

> Her forehead was flower-white; her cheeks like the anemone ruddy-bright; her eyes were those of the wild heifer or the gazelle, with eyebrows like the crescent-moon which ends Sha'abān and begins Ramazān; her mouth was like the ring of Sulayman, her lips coral-red, and her teeth like a line of strung pearls or of camomile petals. Her throat recalled the antelope's, and her breasts, two pomegranates of even size, stood at bay as it were; her body rose and fell in waves below her dress like the rolls of a piece of brocade, and her navel would hold an ounce of benzoin ointment.

This of course recalls the *Song of Songs*, where She has eyes like doves, hair like a flock of goats, teeth like white ewes, belly like a mound of wheat, and breasts like two fawns or clusters of grapes (but He is strictly money: arms like golden scepters with gems of topaz, loins like a throne of ivory inlaid

135

with sapphire, thighs like marble pillars on pedestals of gold).
Or, to take only one example from English poetry, Edmund
Spenser in "Epithalamion":

> Her goodly eyes like Sapphires shining bright,
> Her forehead ivory white,
> Her cheeks like apples which the sun hath rudded,
> Her lips like cherries charming men to bite,
> Her breast like to a bowl of cream uncrudded,
> Her paps like lilies budded,
> Her snowy neck like to a marble tower,
> And all her body like a palace fair,
> Ascending up with many a stately stair,
> To honor's seat and chastity's sweet bower.

Poetry, which looks like a list, has always been susceptible
to list-making. Here, the curiosity of these litanies of similes is
that they are all sensual in their abstract invocation of fertility
(plants, animals, fruit, food) and wealth (ivory, jewels, bro-
cade), but grotesque when specifically imagined: arms like
lotus stalks, mouth like a ring, breasts like grapes or cream
uncrudded, legs like staircases. Thomas Campion's famous
line belongs both to *Immortal Love Poems* and *MAD* magazine:
"There is a garden in her face."

Sometimes whole worlds seem to be contained in the catalog, however brief. A poem from an unspecified Polynesian
island at the turn of the century:

> The rounded cheeks of your buttocks red as the ripe
>   mountain apple,
> Your hair deeply waved like the fronds of the curly-
>   leafed mountain fern,
> Your teeth as white as the heron,
> You are patterned with bands in black and white like
>   the striped fish of the lagoon,
> And your whole body is covered with dotted designs
>   like the eel called Two-lords-gliding-through-the-
>   ocean.

Sometimes the abstract associations have dropped out from the similes, and the world of that beauty seems unrecoverable. An anonymous Chinese poem from the eighth century B.C.E.:

> Hands smooth like rush-down,
> Skin smooth like lard,
> Neck long and white like a tree grub,
> Teeth like melon seeds,
> Cicada's head and moth's eyebrows,
> Smiling a charming smile,
> Her beautiful eyes have the black and white clearly separated.

The most astonishing litany I know is in prose and occurs in the 17th-century Chinese novel *Chin P'ing Mei*. The protagonist, Hsi-men Ch'ing, first catches sight of Golden Lotus, who will become the main female character in the book:

> Her hair was black as a raven's plumage; her eyebrows mobile as the kingfisher and as curved as the new moon. Her almond eyes were clear and cool, and her cherry lips most inviting. Her nose was noble and exquisitely modeled, and her dainty cheeks beautifully powdered. Her face had the delicate roundness of a silver bowl. As for her body, it was as light as a flower, and her fingers as slender as the tender shoots of a young onion. Her waist was as narrow as the willow, and her white belly yielding and plump. Her feet were small and tapering; her breasts soft and luscious. One other thing there was, black-fringed, grasping, dainty, and fresh, but the name of that I may not tell.

The title *Chin P'ing Mei* incorporates the names of the three principal characters, and means "The Plum in the Golden Vase" ("golden vase" also meaning "vagina"), a scene in the book. It was translated in 1939 by Clement Egerton as *The Golden Lotus* with all the salacious passages in Latin (which were not translated into English until 1972). Surely one of the greatest novels, it is an epic of greed, ambition, sex, food, and clothes. Its anonymous author was a disciple of the third century B.C.E. philosopher Hsun-tzu, who expounded the essential evil of mankind and is quoted in the first chapter of the novel: "In this world, only the heart of man is vile." All the characters in the book are bad, except for a few good ones who meet terrible fates. The author scores his philosophical point by making the descriptions of sex, food, and material wealth so detailed and luxurious that the reader is completely caught up—leading to the sudden realization that I, the reader, am as bad as any of these characters.

What is extraordinary in this description—which is followed by two paragraphs on Golden Lotus' clothes, simultaneously dressing and undressing her—is that the love (or lust) at first sight includes a narrative leap to Golden Lotus and Hsi-men Ch'ing as actual lovers. The notorious "mental undressing" of male psychology becomes a fact, not a speculation, and is only modified by a bit of reticence—"the name of that I may not tell"—which, to say the least, hardly exists in the rest of the novel.

Hallmarks of female beauty will, of course, persist forever: the current ones seem to be the collagen-injected lip, the capped tooth, the liposuctioned thigh and flank, the exercise machine-made flat abdomen, and the surgically improved Samoan breast. But the similes for that beauty have vanished. Now a famous beauty (movie star or model) is only "like" another movie star or model, except younger or slightly different. Objective correlatives have become as fleeting as celebrity: the community is too vast, things change too quickly.

Or perhaps the genre was killed off by Baudelaire's passerby, who had eyes as ashen as a cloud before a storm. Walter Benjamin thought the poem—with its unforgettable last line, "I might have loved you and you knew it!"—epitomized the anonymity of the modern city, the essence of which Benjamin captured in a haunting phrase: "love at last sight."

[1999]

IV

KARMIC TRACES

1.

No sooner had the warm liquid, and the crumbs with it, touched my palate than a shudder ran through my whole body, and I stopped, intent upon the extraordinary changes that were taking place. An exquisite pleasure had invaded my senses, but individual, detached, with no suggestion of its origin. And at once the vicissitudes of life had become indifferent to me, its disasters innocuous, its brevity illusory. . .

Its brevity illusory:

"Memory," says Plotinus, "is for those who have forgotten." The gods have no memory because they cannot forget. The gods have no memory because they know no time, have no need to fight against time, have no fragments of what has been lost to recollect, to re-collect. In India, with its vast stretches of time, with its same lives appearing and appearing again, there is no distinction between learning and remembering. You knew it in your past lives, you have always known it, to learn is to re-mind yourself, bring yourself back into the mind of universal knowledge. Says the Jaiminiya Upanishad: "It is the unknown that you should remember." And more: It is the unknown that makes you remember, and its trigger is smell, the *vasana*.

Vasana, which literally means "scent," is karmic residue, the stuff—as ineffable as a smell—that remains from a past life. Each life produces *vasanas*, which remain dormant until one is reincarnated in the same species. That is, the *vasanas* from your life as a cat will only be triggered when, a thousand incarnations later, you are a cat again.

At their most evident, the *vasanas* are responsible for *déjà vu*. In India, you feel you've been here before because you've been here before. The intangible *vasana* is the bridge between those existences. More subtly, you are passionately attracted to another because of the *vasanas* rising from the other, setting

off the memories of your previous love. Every act of love, in
India, is a reenactment.

*. . . I feel something start within me, something that leaves its rest-
ing-place and attempts to rise, something that has been embedded
like an anchor at great depth; I do not know yet what it is, but I can
feel it mounting slowly; I can measure the resistance, I can hear the
echo of great spaces traversed.*

Great spaces traversed:
    Indian erotic poetry is redolent with fragrance. On every
page of the great Sanskrit anthology, Vidyakara's *Treasury*,
compiled a thousand years ago, lovers inhabit an atmosphere
of saffron, sandalwood, human sweat, lotus, mango blossoms,
and the flowers for which there are no translations: garlands
of *bakula*, pink *bandhuka* blossoms, *ketaka* petals bent by bees.
The lovers' mouths are as perfumed as their hair. In Tamil, a
language of South India, the same word means "to be united,
to wed, to embrace" and "to emit fragrance." Conversely, in
the Sanskrit poems, the passion of a lover alone is compared
to a flame burning without any smoke, any smell at all.
    Western science has shown that certain smells, such as
newly mown grass or freshly baked bread, provoke an overwhelming mood of nostalgia—even among those who grew
up on city pavements or associate bread with plastic wrap-
pers. As a catalyst, smell is primary and mysterious: its chemistry makes us not only remember, but want to remember. It is
no coincidence that the most vivid among recent memoirs of
childhood have tended to be written by those who were
raised in extreme poverty or in rural villages, often in the
Third World—places that are sumptuous with smells. Proust
himself thinks his voyage begins with the taste and feel on his
tongue of the madeleine crumbs in the spoon of tea. He men-
tions only in passing, barely notices, their conjunction with
the fragrant steam rising from the cup.
    We in the American middle class grew up in a world
almost entirely devoid of smells, except for that of household
cleaning products, and barely remember our childhoods at all,
except for the television programs. And worse, Protestantism

has given us no neutral word, like "taste," for smell. "Stench" or "fragrance" are exact, as they should be, but "odor" or "smell," which should have no value, generally imply a foulness, and "to smell" misleadingly is both a transitive and intransitive verb. They pertain to a world whose Satan has a smell, but whose God does not.

And the scientists now say that "the brain has two memory systems, one for ordinary information and one for emotionally charged information." That is, information that occurs under some form of stress, set off by the ancient evolutionary "fight or flight" reaction, is created by the adrenergic hormones, adrenaline and noradrenaline, and stored in the amygdala, "a pair of walnut-shaped structures that regulate emotion." The *vasanas*, say certain commentators, are specifically the memory-traces of powerful desires: among them, the desire for fame or respectability, erotic desire, the desire for knowledge gained from books, spiritual longing. And it is desire, always the need for more, that leads you to be born over and over into this world you crave.

But desire, as it is recognized in India, is also a kind of forgetting. There is a Sanskrit word, *durdhara*, that means both "irresistible" and "difficult to remember." The word is practically a poem itself, but it is made tangible in a lyric by the 8th-century poet Vidya, the earliest surviving woman poet in Sanskrit:

> What wealth,
> that you can chatter
> about a night spent
> with your lover—
> the teasings,
> smiles, whispered words—
> even his special fragrance.
> Because O my friends I swear—
> from the moment
> my lover's hand touched my
> skirt, I remember
> nothing at all.
>
> (trans. Andrew Schelling)

The lover, irresistible and difficult to remember. Vidya's friends can remember the fragrance that attracted them to their lovers. But her passion, according to her, was even greater, erasing the traces of the *vasana* that created it. We read her as earthy; in India she would also be metaphysical: the passion of which there is no memory, that comes from no memory, is an act of Tantrism: a release from, an obliteration of, the illusory world.

But when from a long-distant past nothing subsists, after the people are dead, after the things are broken and scattered, still, alone, more fragile, but with more vitality, more unsubstantial, more persistent, more faithful, the smell and taste of things remain poised a long time, like souls, ready to remind us, waiting and hoping for their moment, amid the ruins of all the rest; and bear unfaltering, in the tiny and almost impalpable drop of their essence, the vast structure of recollection.

The structure of recollection:

2.

I was in a cab going across Tenth Street. Cars were parked on either side, half illegally, leaving only one lane open. In the middle of the block, the car in front of us, a washed and polished red compact, stopped. It didn't move. Nothing was blocking it; no sign of engine trouble, the ignition turning over; and no way to get around it. We sat. The cabbie, a Bangladeshi, looked at me in the rearview mirror, raised his eyebrows, and shrugged. He didn't speak; perhaps it was the heat. Cars backed up behind us, but no one honked. It was August in a long summer; no one could take it anymore; I had a train to catch.

I got out of the cab to look. The windows of the red car were rolled up. At the wheel was a nondescript man, the sort one takes to be a computer programmer, maybe thirty, pudgy, short hair, a clean white shirt, glasses. I gestured, in the way they do here, Hey buddy what's the problem? He didn't look up. I yelled louder, waved my arms. He turned. He smiled, kept smiling, and slowly rubbed his finger across the side of his nose, over and over. I stared; he smiled; he rubbed his nose; I got back in the cab; we sat; no one honked. The block, it seemed, had stopped dead.

You look in the rearview mirror, you hear yourself breathe, you hear your voice, some voice speaking, it's hot, you are alive. And alive at this century's end, a middle-class man in a capital of the West, is to be adrift. You're late, everyone's always late, watching the imaginary train recede into the tunnel. They say, I don't know what happened to the time. They mean, I don't know what happened to time.

Time had speeded up and danced itself to exhaustion. Speed was the century's novelty and its glamour: cars, planes, rockets, computer calculations, and instantaneous communication. Filmed and written narratives leapt from point to point without transitions, running as memory runs, and in the end forgot there was a story to tell. Past the gate of Apollinaire's "Zone" every poem written was an exercise in (or deliberate rejection of) simultaneity. Long poems—Eliot's *The Waste Land* or Huidobro's *Altazor*—kept reminding the reader to hurry up. Every Western language cut back the vines of its rhetorical flourishes. Who had the time? Attention shortened; you were too busy; everything took too long, and was hard to remember later.

Time had slowed down and petrified. Muybridge, with his studies of human and animal locomotion, put the brakes on; the motion picture camera brought motion to a halt. Each fraction of a second in the movement of time was frozen. Or, like Zeno's arrow, time itself was a series of frame replacing motionless frame. What the camera saw, the bullet entering the apple, was real. What the eye saw, the apple exploding, was not. The 19th-century photograph of an isolated subject became the 20th-century photograph of the isolated fraction of time, a "decisive moment" in a milieu of general indecision. Frames full of life that saw the life we perpetually had just missed catching.

Time had stretched out to the unimaginable distances of light traveling to the speculated end of the universe, if the universe had an end, if the universe had a beginning. Time, in a black hole, vanished. Time, at the speed of light, went backwards. Time, among the subatomic particles, had no forwards. It was said: Consider the fruit fly, which lives and dies in a day. Born on a winter morning, it knows only a frozen world; a hundred generations later only the heat; a hundred more must pass until the world of the ancestors returns. Western time became Hindu time: a million human years a blink of an eye of a god who lives a life of a million god-years each in a series of a million births and rebirths.

Time kept jumping off the track. Forgotten acquaintances came to mind and then suddenly appeared on the corner. I saw a friend's black eye a few hours before the accident occurred; I dreamt obituaries in the morning newspaper the night before they were published. For some years, for no reason, I could unerringly predict the sex of unborn babies; then, for no reason, I lost it. All of us heard the phone ring before it rang; all of us knew, at times, who was calling.

[In *An Experiment with Time*, a book from the 1920's that Borges loved, the author devises an ingenious method for proving that time is an infinity of perpendicular lines. The main narratives of dreams are irrelevant; one must carefully note the small details. For example, you may dream that you are making love to your sister. It does not matter. But remember the curious bibelot lying on the bedside table next to you in the dream. Tomorrow you will see that same object in the flea market.]

Time seemed to have lost its shape. Bergson, opening the century, had said it was a mistake to confuse time with space. But what mind could not think of time as a river flowing by, a road leading to the end of the road? If time was no longer the circle of the ancients, the revolution of rising and falling eras that would return, then it was at least the straight track of progress, pushing forward in the name of the perfectibility of humankind. Upheaval launched it, dreams set the course, but injustice propelled it, and it crashed in another upheaval. Time was going nowhere. Things were a little better and a lot worse. In the ruins of the city another city was built, and then another, and another, none more golden than any other.

What had happened to time? We were in a hurry, spend-
ing our time waiting. As a child, I was required to sit under
my desk at school, bent over, hands locked behind my neck,
to practice waiting for the atomic bomb. I grew up waiting,
always on the verge of what would happen, in the perpetual
present of being alive in the penultimate moment of the end
of time.

We look at each other, amazed that we've aged.

3.

Time then, or how we inhabit it, has taken on the condition of
poetry. A poem belongs to an historical moment, fixed by time
and place, most evident in the language the poem speaks, but
also in its range of concerns and the form—its clothes of fashion—in which the poem is wrapped. But it simultaneously
exists outside of the historical continuum. Ancient poems, the
great ones, are as immediate, or more immediate, than those
written yesterday. Some indefinable living matter in the
poem—perhaps it is its karmic traces—allows it to remain
vital as it persists through the ages, even as the language in
which it was written dies out, even as it travels by translation
from language to language.

At the end of a century that has dismantled all the old
models of time, we too, in everyday life, tend more and more
to explain the present tense, our ordinary activities and emo-
tions, by some distant timeless factor. How often we hear that
I am the way I am because of the arrangement of the stars and
planets according to the Babylonian cosmology, because of
traits programmed in the genes to ensure the survival of
hominids, because of traumas in infancy, or the traumas of
one's ancestors in history. However ludicrous these reversions
to an original determining principle sometimes are, they
reflect a universal human desire for an origin, and a coherent
narrative of what has happened since, a continuity of the
ancient and the new.

In all of the world's origin myths, the universe comes
together. Our supposedly scientific version may be the first
time a culture has created a story of the creation based on a

perpetual disjunction: after the primary explosion, the pieces of the universe hurtling forever farther apart from each other. It is a sentiment most of us may well feel in our daily lives, but it has turned out, though some have tried, to be no rock on which to build a church. A religion, or an ideology, presumes to provide the answers, not compound the questions that led to its creation.

As the scientists invent increasingly precise instruments for measuring the universe, the universe itself has become even more mysterious. Never has a culture known more and understood less. Just the other day, some physicists announced that, according to their calculations, 90% of all the matter in the universe is missing. The problem would not have occurred in Dante's Florence or among the Yekuana of the Orinoco, but we, readers of modernist fragments and "field" compositions from Mallarmé to Olson, have grown accustomed to it. Things float—like the earth first seen from the moon—alone and surrounded by nothing. For us in the West, the models of the ancient and the cosmic are now as various, unconnected, and contradictory as the ideas and things we confront in the local present. It is a condition of endless dialectic with no syntheses, no idea of a future, and where—never more than now—the only ardent believers left are those who know nothing.

4.

I sat under my desk, hands locked behind my neck, waiting for doom. I grew up, like a child in a cult, on the cliff's edge, gazing down, transfixed, and later an expert, even a connoisseur, of the apocalypses, the time bombs mankind had set for itself.

The planes of the Strategic Air Command, armed, always airborne, every minute of the year somewhere aloft and waiting. The nuclear submarines, armed, submerged for six months at a stretch, somewhere down there waiting. The missiles in the silos, enough of them that new targets had to be invented, small provincial capitals; enough of them to obliterate the planet seven times in succession. Enough of them. And the indelible movies of the miscellaneous and crazed survivors, even Fred Astaire, undancing, under the banner "There's Still Time Brother." Sex, in adolescent dreams, was located then not in a place but a time: shipwrecked with the inamorata not on a desert island, but in the last half-hour of the planet.

It never happened, and time stretched out into slow doom. Now there was time for the canisters of plutonium to rot on the ocean floor, the deserts expand, the forests fall, the acidic rain fall, the species diminish one by one, the reactor core melt down, the ozone to scatter in the upper atmosphere, a riddled shield against malevolent rays, and the ozone to grow thick in the lower atmosphere, a counterpane to melt the poles. A population that had doubled since my birth, that will have doubled again at my actuarially predicted death; four of me where once was me; more me's than all the me's that ever lived, me's, presumably, with the transmigrated souls of ants.

It was a doom of ants, the doom of the proliferation of malevolent ordinary things. The aerosol spray cans destroying the upper atmosphere. The video terminals, where the new masses sit day after day, causing tumors and miscarriages. The countless gadgets of late capitalism—the toasters, hair dryers, clothes dryers, electric razors, blenders—emitting electromagnetic pulses that mutate cells. And the story that appeared on the front page and was never seen again: that paper, all paper—the book you hold on your lap—is drenched with dioxin, the most potent of the carcinogens.

Food, above all, is the source of dread: pesticides, fat, hormones, cholesterol, additives. Every snack has become the glass of milk Cary Grant brings up the stairs to Joan Fontaine in *Suspicion*, gleaming like an evil star. In the supermarkets the shoppers are stopped in their tracks, reading the ingredients lists on the packages, searching for signs of harm like detectives, Roman priests, or the insane.

From Benjamin's age of mechanical reproduction where art objects lost the aura of their uniqueness: to the television age where electronically reproduced representations of reality caused reality to lose its aura, flattened into a succession of images flashing past the viewer with a remote control button:

to an age where the aura, albeit an evil aura, has indeed returned to illuminate the everyday objects of mechanical reproduction. The mundane is saturated with malevolence; the pure products of America have gone crazy. Surrealism has become inadvertently prophetic: Lorca's "assassinated by the sky" is now as literal as Man Ray's spiked clothes iron. There is even now a new theory for the Ice Age. Not the slow southward crawl of the glaciers: One day, they say, it started snowing, and it just never stopped.

5.

In classical China, every act of writing began as an act of reading. Lu Chi's *Wen Fu*, an extraordinary *ars poetica* written in the 3rd century, opens with the poet "standing at the center of things, observing in the darkness, nourishing his feelings and his intellect on the great works of the past." After meditating on the passage of the seasons, then on time itself, then on all the things of the world, he "sings of the blazing splendor of the moral power of his predecessors, wanders in the forest of letters and among the treasure houses of literary works, admiring the perfect balance of their intricate and lovely craft." And then "moved, he puts aside his books and picks up his writing-brush," in order, as Lu Chi says, "to make it manifest in literature."

Fourteen hundred years later, the 17th-century Chinese critic, Yeh Hsieh, in his treatise *The Origin of Poetry*, comments: "When what I write is the same as what a former master wrote, it means that we were one in our reflections. And when I write something different from former masters, I may be filling in something missing from their work. Or it is possible that the former masters are filling in something missing in my work."

This sense of the past has little to do with the Western idea of "tradition," as it has been used for the last two thousand years, and which has always been based on a reversion to older (often forgotten or obscured) models. (Its latest incarnation, in the United States, is the so-called New Formalist insistence on a return to 19th-century prosody.) It has even less to do with the current legend of the "anxiety of influence," where the act of writing is reduced to the mating habits of elks, the elder and younger males with their great antlers clashing. For some 2,500 years in Chinese poetry, the tradition meant transmission: continual change in a past that was moving steadily forward. Those who would go back, the slavish imitators of the past, are always derided in Chinese criticism. On the other hand, Chinese poetry, until this century, knew none of the dramatic ruptures of style and content that have been normal in the West. The Chinese poem, written in a language that changed slowly and was centuries behind its spoken equivalent, filled with skillful allusions to other poems, was seen as one more piece in an unending dialogue between the living and the dead. In the West, tradition means that the living modify the dead. In China, one might say that the dead revise their own poems through the living.

Sanskrit poetics applied the theory of karmic traces to the act of reading. One responds to a poem because it speaks directly to one's experience, but that experience need not have occurred in this life. An inexperienced student is moved by an erotic poem because of the karmic traces of ancient loves. Similarly—and unusually compassionately for pedagogues— it is said that if a student is unmoved by a poem, it is due to insufficiencies and accumulated demerit in his previous lives. (Luckily, little distinction is made between experience and poetry: If, for example, one knows nothing of love from this or previous lives, one can learn of love—and create the karmic traces of love for future lives—through the deep emotional study of poetry, a study that is specifically described as not technical, grammatical, or pedantic.)

Poetry, then, in India, is not only the place where we may hear the dead speak, it is the place where we hear our dead selves speak. There is not our wonder that the ancient words still move us, nor our recourse to the explanation, which is partially untrue, that human experience is universal and ahistorical. But although Sanskrit poetics has much to say about the *vasanas* of reading, it has nothing that I know of about the *vasanas* of writing. For clearly, in the Indian cosmos, the act of

writing, like any other act, must involve older versions of the
one who currently moves the pen.

6.

After the fall of the Aztec empire in 1519, and after the deci-
mating plagues of 1520, 1531, and the worst from 1545 to 1548,
in the years approximately from 1550 to 1570, after the long
night of the conquest and an hour before the dawn of an institutionalized Spanish empire, the survivors were swept up in
the cult of the performance of a spectacle called the Netotilitzi.
Artaud would have loved it: a stage, hazy with incense, decorated with flowers and artificial trees; dancers adorned with
feathers and paint and flowers; warriors reenacting battles
with fans and crooks; boys dressed as birds and butterflies,
sucking the dew from the flowers; singers and musicians
playing all night on gourd rattles, rasps, conches, reed flutes,
gongs, bells and jingles, clay whistles, log drums, skin drums
and turtle shell drums.

The songs they sang in the Netotilitzi were written down
through native informants by the priests, who collected these
things both in fascination and as evidence of local depravity
(much as the religious right now compiles archives of pornography). Sometime after 1585, after the cult had disappeared,
the songs were recopied and collected under the title *Cantares
Mexicanos*, "Mexican Songs." They form a strange, ultimately
inexplicable text: ninety-one songs or chants written in a
metaphorical language that was probably incomprehensible
to its audience. The first complete translation of the book was
published only ten years ago. The translator, John Bierhorst,
had succeeded after two previous Nahuatl scholars had died
midway though their own versions.

It is Bierhorst's theory that the Netotilitzi spectacle was
part of a ghost dance cult, similar to the one that swept the
Plains Indians in North America in the 1870's and ended
twenty years later with the massacre at Wounded Knee. But
whereas the Plains ghost dance songs were meant to summon
the warriors back to earth to defeat the white people, the
Cantares were something quite different: These songs were not

the invention of their singers, directed to the dead. These songs were taken to be the dead warriors themselves; that is, the dead warriors having been coaxed back to earth with offerings of food, flowers, music, and sex, now appeared transformed into songs to right the world. Even more, they brought a taste of paradise, for these song-ghosts, on arrival here, simultaneously transported their singers to the other world.

Reading poetry is one place where we get the chance to listen to the dead. Writing it, in the West, we can talk back to them. In China, the dead talk through us. In India our own dead selves can speak. On the North American Plains and in many other cultures, it was a way to summon the dead. In the Aztec spectacle, the poem itself was an avenging ghost.

George Oppen, in a letter, said of a mediocre poet that he was not afraid enough of poetry.

7.

There is a substance in the brain called N,N-dimethyltryptamine (DMT) whose function is unknown. Synthesized in the 1930's and later worked on by Albert Hoffmann, the begetter of LSD, DMT was known as one of the ingredients of the psychoactive snuffs and the brew called *ayahuasca* used by shamans in the Amazon. Yet, in the psychedelic era, DMT had a reputation, largely promoted by William Burroughs, as the most terrifying drug in the pharmacopeia, and few dared try it. Lately it has been rediscovered, and its clandestine researchers have been writing some strange laboratory notes.

Nearly all describe similar experiences. Smoked or injected, the drug takes almost immediate effect, and the whole "trip" lasts only fifteen minutes. First one hears an intense ripping sound, as though one's head is being torn apart. Then one sees a series of vivid geometric patterns, followed by a sense of hurtling through a tunnel or wall or membrane, and finally breaking through to a defined place that has nothing to distinguish it, but which seems underground and possibly vaulted. In this place, one encounters beings who are neither anthropomorphic nor zoomorphic, yet are clearly alive. They are performing actions that are incomprehensible, and speaking or singing in a language that can be sensed but not understood—that is, those who think they have understood something have been unable to articulate what it is.

The universality of this experience under DMT of an encounter with beings has set off—this is, after all, the drug world—flurries of odd speculation. That DMT exists in the brain to act as a communications link. That the beings inhabit a parallel reality. That one has somehow traveled into the cells, the atoms, or the subatomic particles. That the beings are extraterrestrials, inhabiting or exploring our world, but otherwise invisible to us. That they represent some sort of program which, when we are "advanced" enough to understand it, will allow us to contact the extraterrestrials (who, some would add, created us in the first place). Or that, less elaborately, these entities are simply the souls of the dead. The explanations are fanciful, if not ridiculous, but do not necessarily discredit the evidence. Humans, as is well known, have poor powers of sense perception compared to most of the animal and insect kingdom. Psychotropic drugs have traditionally been used to broaden the band of what may be perceived. So why not assume for a moment that the reports are accurate, that there really is something, some things, there?

It is nearly a universal belief, among poets, that someone else writes what they write. The Greek and Roman poets, of course, attributed their words to the Muses; the poets of many other societies credited their own local divinities. (An ignorant peasant, Vyasa, became the author of the longest poem in the world, the *Mahabarata*, only because of his devotion to Krishna; God gave Cædmon, a shepherd, his poems in a dream.) The Romantics thought of themselves as Aeolian harps, played by the wind. In this century, this metaphor was transformed into that of the radio: the poet is the antenna, receiving the words from out of the air. Similarly, the most documented New World shaman, María Sabina, a Mazatec from Oaxaca who was illiterate, claimed that, under the influence of hallucinogenic mushrooms, she was a given a book from which she read her songs.

[In English, at least, it is only with the rise of Protestantism that the image shifts from divine inspiration to the poet as "maker," a craftsman of words. Rejected by the self-consciously pagan Romantics, it returns with the technology-inspired Modernists: William Carlos Williams' image of the poem as a "machine made of words," Pound's famous dictum that "poetry must be as well-written as prose." It is a kind of Calvinist work ethic of poetry that few cultures have shared, and one which persists these days as the belief that poetry is a "craft" that can be learned in a "workshop."]

Octavio Paz, in a poem, sees an old man on a bench talking to himself, and asks parenthetically, "Whom do we talk to/ when we talk to ourselves?" The question is not entirely flip. If poetry, as Paz has written, is the "other voice" of society, the voice that is other to the norms and fashions, the voice that often says what the society does not want to hear, it is also true that, according to the poets, the poem is written or spoken in a voice that is "other" to the poet's own. But who, then, is speaking?

The reflexive verbs of spiritual and psychological quests, and of utterly ordinary life—*I lost myself, I found myself, I saw myself, I told myself, I thought to myself that I was losing touch with myself*—assume a dialogue between speakers: The human mind may be the only one, among the animals, that can observe and describe itself. In the scientific age, this has become inexplicable. Most other cultures, however, saw no mystery in it at all.

People have nearly always believed that each of us is inhabited by at least two beings, a self that lives and dies, and a something-else that is timeless: a soul, a spirit, an unconscious that may even be collective. [The more "primitive" the society, the more complex and numerous these essences are. A Khond in the jungles of Orissa in east India—to take one example—has four souls. One soul belongs to the gods and joins them at death; one belongs to the tribe and is reborn in another tribal member; one belongs to the individual and dies with its owner; and one belongs to the forest and is reborn as a tiger.] Consciousness is the conjunction of an observer, usually timeless and immaterial, and an observed that is fixed in

a body in time. Unlike Rimbaud's famous "I is another," I are
an us. In moments of extreme stress, the two dramatically separate: Those who have almost died report looking down on
themselves from the ceiling as they lie in bed, an experience
that is routine for shamans and common for anybody under
hallucinogens. Even in an ordinary moment, if we bother to
think of it, we know exactly what we look like as we do what
we are doing, sitting in a chair reading, or sitting in a chair
typing. But who is watching whom?

The Buddha taught that the way to achieve enlightenment
was to erase all the *vasanas*, all the memories and traces of old
desires. Pythagoras, conversely, taught that the way to escape
the cycle of rebirths was to systematically remember everything that had happened in all of one's previous lives. Either
state—knowing all or forgetting all—is divine and not human.

The gods, of course, do not write poetry. The poem is produced by that encounter between the two worlds, or two
halves of the world: in time and out of time, in the body and
out of the body, in the individual and in the collective of history, the particular culture, and humanity itself. And the poem
itself is both a metaphor and an embodiment of the process of
its own creation: The poet dies, the biographical facts are lost,
and the poem remains. The language changes, meanings drop
out, and the poem remains. The language is no longer spoken,
the city in which it was written is a buried ruin, and the poem
remains. And stranger still: the ultimately indescribable
essence, or being, or quality, that endures in the poem is precisely that which engenders, becomes embodied in, the next
poem. There is a karma of poetry: The best poems lead thousands of subsequent lives as other poems, what Robert Duncan
called the Great Collage. And perhaps the bad poems are
reborn as that which they resembled in their lives as bad
poems: entries in a diary, embarrassing love letters, self-pub-
lished memoirs, anecdotal "filler" stories at the bottom of
columns in provincial newspapers, descriptive passages in
tedious travel accounts, suicide notes that were not followed by
suicide, song lyrics for which no one will ever write the music.

I was stuck in a cab on Tenth Street. The driver, a Bangladeshi, was dozing, or perhaps he, too, had let his mind wander with no purpose. Time wasn't passing, it had stopped. The sidewalks were empty; the cars behind us sat in silence. Suddenly, for no apparent reason, the red compact car began moving down the block. Life started up again. We overtook him at the corner, raising our middle fingers and yelling obscenities. The clean and pudgy driver waved back with a smile. Artaud had said that a writer should be like the victim, tied to the stake, who signals through the flame. But perhaps the writer is an anonymous man making incomprehensible gestures, silent behind plate glass, who is capable of stopping time. We rushed on to the station where—I can't explain this—I hadn't missed my train.

[1995]

THE FALLS

"Black and hideous to me is the tragedy that gathers, and I'm sick beyond cure to have lived to see it. You and I, the ornaments of our generation, should have been spared this wreck of our belief that through the long years we had seen civilization grow and the worst become impossible. The tide that bore us along was then all the while moving to this as its grand Niagara yet what a blessing we didn't know it."

—Henry James, letter to Rhoda Broughton,
August 1914

1.

In the second millennium B.C.E., the coast of Palestine is known as Kinahna, for the people there make a purple dye called *kinahhu* from the shells on the beach. In the 12th century B.C.E., the land is conquered by the Philistines coming east from across the sea and the Hebrews ("the people from over there") coming west from the desert. The people of Kinahna, and all the other subjugated groups of the region—Amorites, Hivites, Perizzites, Girgashites, and Jebusites, among them—become known indiscriminately as Kinahnites, the Canaanites.

Around the year 1000 B.C.E., in the time of David and Solomon, the Hebrews begin to codify the tale of their origin in what would later become the Book of Genesis. The beautiful story of the Covenant of the Rainbow is immediately followed by a bizarre anecdote: Noah is lying in his tent, drunk and naked; his son Ham walks in and accidentally sees him; he tells his brothers, Shem and Japheth, who are outside; they take a blanket and, walking backwards, not looking, cover Noah. When Noah wakes, he levels a curse, not at Ham, but at one of Ham's sons, Canaan. Canaan will be a slave of slaves to his brothers. Shem is blessed and Canaan will be his slave. Japheth will dwell in the tents of Shem and Canaan will be his slave.

The Hebrews believe that they are Semites, the descendants of Shem. The Canaanites—all the conquered indigenous peoples—descend from Canaan. As it is apparent that the Hebrews will be unable to defeat the Philistines, and must share the land with them, the Philistines become the heirs of Japheth, dwelling, however, in the tents of Shem.

The Canaanites are slaves, but over the centuries, as they convert to the Hebrew god or bear the children of Hebrew patriarchs or are freed by their masters and acquire wealth, they become indistinguishable from the Hebrews. Slaves are then imported from abroad, depending on wars and political fortunes: Syrians or Egyptians or Ethiopians or Cushites or, much later, in the medieval period, the displaced victims of the tribal wars in the Caucusus or in the Balkans. For two thousand years, all are known in the Jewish Levant, at one time or another, as Canaanites, the descendants of Ham.

There are slaves in every era, and—except for criminals or the disastrously impoverished—slaves are ethnic others, conquered or devastated peoples. (Only in Muscovy were Russian slaves Russian.) Because they are others and because they are slaves, they become known as a slavish people: stupid, lazy, promiscuous, childlike, drunken, dishonest. They are treated like animals, therefore they are like animals; they are clothed in rags and not permitted to wash, therefore they are a ragged, dirty people who smell bad. Slavery, a fate of vulnerable aliens, nearly always becomes a hereditary condition, applicable until history enslaves another group.

The Romans have red-haired Thracian slaves, so red hair becomes a sign of slavishness and Rufus (Redhead) the typical slave name; actors on the Roman stage playing slaves wear red wigs. In the classical period, Gauls and Britons, among others, are slaves and slavish peoples. As the Britons and Gauls become English and French, the slaves and the slavish come from the Caucasus, and Caucasians are the substandard people. In the late Middle Ages, the Balkans supply the slaves; in most of the Western European languages, the word "slave"

derives from "Slav," as does the Arabic word for eunuch and
the Spanish word for a link of chain.

The Bible preaches a single family of mankind descended
from Adam and Eve, and punishes those who discriminate
racially. When Moses' sister Miriam objects to his marriage to
Zipporah, a black Cushite, Yahweh turns her "leprous, white
as snow"; pure white is a sign of sickliness. The Queen of
Sheba is celebrated for her blackness and beauty; the universality of Christ is demonstrated by the black Magus bringing
a gift at the birth.

The first Christians were largely recruited from freed slaves,
and Christianity, in its first thousand years, has an ambiguous
relation to slavery. All Christians are "slaves of Christ." It is
better to be a slave, says St. Paul, than to be free, for the suffering of the slave will be rewarded in the next life. All men,
says St. Augustine, are miserable sinners and thus deserving
of slavery. Isidore of Seville says it is a just chastisement for
sin. Through the Middle Ages, the slaves of Europe are white.
Christians are allowed to have Christian slaves.

In the Middle East, although there had been slaves from south
of the Sahara as far back as the Egyptian Middle Kingdom,
they remain a small minority. However, as the only visible
blacks are slaves, a tradition slowly begins in the third or
fourth centuries C.E. that blacks are slavish, and therefore the
descendants of Ham. Jewish myths are constructed that turn
Ham black. In one of them, Ham, like the dog and the crow,
copulates on the Ark, where it is forbidden, and turns black.
In another, Noah's curse is, "Your seed will be ugly and dark-
skinned." [In 1696, Hermann von der Hardt would suggest
that to "see the nakedness" of one's father means to have
incestuous relations with one's mother; Canaan is cursed
because he is the son of Ham and Noah's wife.]

The Qur'an preaches a universal brotherhood of the faithful
and makes no racial discrimination. Arabs believe they are
Semites because they trace their origins to Ishmael,

Abraham's son and Isaac's brother. (Thus Jews and Arabs are cousins.) In the first centuries of Islam, the Arabic term *Banu Ham*, "Sons of Ham," is applied to the Egyptians, Persians, and Berbers, until their conversion. Under Islamic law, no Muslim or Jew or Christian under Muslim protection can become a slave. The rise of Arab trade routes to black Africa, which is fragmented in small and often mutually hostile groups eager to collaborate in the depopulation of their enemies, turns the sub-Sahara into the primary source of slaves in the Mediterranean during the Muslim hegemony.

By the year 1000, *Banu Ham* becomes a synonym for black Africans. The Persian historian al-Tabari writes: "Ham begot all blacks and people with crinkly hair; Japheth all who have broad faces and small eyes [the Turkic peoples]; and Shem all who have beautiful faces and beautiful hair." The Persians, once Hamites, have now become Semites. The Jews similarly identify Ham and blacks, but in Christian Europe, which has almost no black slaves, the Children of Ham remain white: from country to country, they are merely the current subjugated others.

By around 1100, with the solidification of the feudal order and the rise of serfdom, slavery as a local practice in western and northern Europe begins to vanish slowly, but Christians continue to sell Christian slaves to Muslim and Jewish traders for the Muslim markets. Castrated slaves are particularly in demand, but Jews and Muslims will not perform castration, so this is done by the Christians themselves.

With the First Crusade, Europe becomes mad for sugar; huge plantations are set up in the eastern Mediterranean. With the expulsion of the Crusaders, the sugar industry moves westward: Cyprus, Crete, Sicily, southern Spain, Madeira, the Canaries—and later to the New World. Plantations require masses of cheap labor; these are, at first, manned by Slavic slaves and refugees from the religious wars. But the fall of Constantinople to the Turks, and the rise of Ivan the Great and Russian state power, effectively cuts the supply of slaves from the Black Sea. Slaves must be imported from the south. In the 15th century, the powerless and peasant peoples of sub-Saharan Africa are besieged on two sides. From the east, Sudanese Islamic chiefs declare a holy war against the *kaffirs*, the unbelievers, who are captured and sold. From the West, Portuguese slave traders raid the coast.

Americas: The indigenous peoples, decimated by the new European diseases, make poor slaves. White slaves fare badly in the tropics. Black slaves live relatively longer and are a better investment. The languages of Africa are so diverse that few aboard ship can communicate with one another, preventing conspiracy and rebellion. A favorable trade wind blows from Guinea to the New World: the Middle Passage.

Twelve million are captured in Africa between 1500 and 1870; a million and a half die in the crossing, another two million within a year of arrival. By the 18th century, blacks become, almost universally, the Canaanites, the Children of Ham, the new Slavs, the slavish people, and Noah's curse becomes a primary defense of their enslavement in the centuries of debate, in both Western Europe and the New World, over slavery. But in Istanbul and other parts of the eastern Mediterranean, as late as the eve of World War I, both black and white slaves are still sold on the blocks.

2.

The problem is reconciling the newly discovered peoples of the Americas with Biblical genealogy. Persuaded by Bartolomé de las Casas, the Church in 1537 recognizes the American Indians as *veri homines*, true men, capable of receiving the True Faith. But where did these true men come from? Giordano Bruno says there were three ancestors of mankind— Enoch, Leviathan, and Adam—and that Adam was the patriarch only of the Jews. (Christopher Marlowe and Thomas Hariot, among others, agree.) Marc Lescarbot says that Noah himself had sailed to Brazil and populated it. Arguments are put forth in favor of Romans, Greeks, Phoenicians, Chinese,

Egyptians, Africans, Ethiopians, French, Tartars, Cambrians, Kurlanders, Frisians, Scyths, and the Atlanteans of the lost continent. Hugo Grotius, in exile in Sweden, maintains they are Swedish.

In Peru in 1590, José de Acosta proposes that the American Indians belong to the ten Lost Tribes of Israel, and are therefore the Children of Shem, who crossed to the New World by some as-yet-undiscovered land bridge. This is enthusiastically endorsed by the Jews scattered or forced into conversion by the Inquisition, and it is spread in Holland and England by the powerful Rabbi Manasseh ben Israel. In his 1650 book, *The Hope of Israel*, Manasseh writes that he had once met a man in Amsterdam named Montezinus, a Jew, who told this story: In America, he had encountered some Indians who, learning that he was Jewish, took him to meet a tribe of Jews. They traveled for days in the wilderness until they came to a river. There, three men and a woman in a boat greeted him: "*Shema, yisrael, adonai elohenu, adonai ehad.*" They quoted the Ten Commandments, but did not allow Montezinus to cross the river to their village.

Manasseh notes the many customs that Jews and Indians have in common: They rend their clothes in sorrow; they celebrate jubilees; they divorce unfaithful wives; they punish the sodomist; they marry their brother's widow; they remember the Flood. Roger Williams in Rhode Island adds another to the list: "They constantly and strictly separate their women in a little Wigwam by themselves in their feminine seasons."

Sir Hamon L'Estrange in 1652 says the Indians are indeed descended from Shem, but they are not Jews. No Jew is permitted to marry a whore, and all Indian women are whores. No Jew may eat unclean meat, but Indians will eat anything.

Three years later, in one of the most controversial books of the century, Isaac de la Peyrere subjects Genesis to some common sense in order to disprove the Semitic origins of the Indians: Adam was merely the father of the Jews alone; there were many others who had already been created and already living in cities, for where did Cain find the knife that slew Abel, and where did he find his wife? The Flood had only covered Palestine: How else could the dove return with an olive branch, for otherwise the trees would have been rotted and destroyed? Given the 3,000 years since the Flood, how else could the entire globe have been populated so quickly? And so on.

[First calculated by Theophilus of Antioch in the second century, it is known that the earth is about 6,000 years old. Refined by Joseph Justus Scaliger in 1583 and Dionysius Patavius in 1627, the chronology is definitively fixed by James Ussher, Archbishop of Armagh and Primate for All Ireland, in the 1650's. Heaven and earth were created on Saturday night, October 23rd, 4004 B.C.E.; the angels were created the following Sunday morning to sing praise to the Lord. The Flood occurred 1656 years after the Creation; Noah and the animals entered the ark on December 7th, 2349 B.C.E. On May 6th the ark came to rest on Mount Ararat, and on December 18th, a Thursday, they were all finally able to leave. In the 1770's, the French begin to suggest that the six days of Creation may be allegorical, and that the earth may be far older. The English, however, reject this as another revolutionary and destabilizing idea from France, and for another century would insist on the Ussher chronology, attributing all geological phenomena to the effects of the Flood.]

In certain pockets, the American Indians as a lost tribe of Israel would remain an inspiration into the 19th century; the story is a central motif of the angelically written golden tablets that would become *The Book of Mormon*. But it was clearly a belief that was not useful to the policies of displacement and extermination that accompanied the westward expansion. Moreover, the English had a tradition that they themselves were the heirs of Shem (unlike most Europeans, who ascribed their lineage to Japheth). Proposed by the Venerable Bede, continued by Geoffrey of Monmouth and the medieval copyists, and later subscribed to by Milton, Cromwell, Blake, and Queen Victoria, among many others, the English saw themselves as either the direct descendants of the Israelites—having, in ancient times, taken refuge on the island, and therefore of purer blood than the present-day Jews—or, thanks to a reinterpretation of certain Scriptural passages, as their replacement as God's chosen people. England, as in Blake's poem and the subsequent hymn, was the new Jerusalem. Thus the continuing insistence that England is different from, and not part of, Europe; a greater relative tolerance, historically, for Jews; and the rumor that royal males have always been circumcised.

3.

Races: In 1666, Georgius Hornius says there are three: Japhetites (white), Semites (yellow), and Hamites (black).

In 1684, François Bernier says there are four: Europeans, who include Egyptians, Indians, and American Indians ("their color is only accidental and is due merely to the fact that they are exposed to the sun"); Africans ("their blackness is essential"); Chinese and Japanese ("flat faces, hidden noses, and small, pig-like eyes"); and Laplanders ("these are vile animals").

The Comte de Buffon, in his 1749 *Natural History,* declares that the non-white peoples are merely degenerate forms of white people, caused by climate. He recommends, as an experiment, transplanting a group of Danes to Senegal and a group of Senegalese to Denmark, keeping them isolated for generations, and seeing whether their physical characteristics change.

In 1774, *Long's History of Jamaica* by Edward Long, notes three races: Europeans and related groups, Negroes, and Orang-Outangs. The popularity of the book—it will be cited for decades—may be due to its speculations about the couplings of the latter two: "I do not think an Orang-Outang would be any dishonor to an Hottentot female."

In the 18th century, American Indians, like Tahitians, are Noble Savages; Africans merely savages. The union of white and red produces a *mestizo,* a mixed person; the union of white and black produces a *mulatto,* a mule-like person; and it is widely believed that mulattoes, like mules, are sterile.

In 1776, the birth of the United States coincides with the birth of the Caucasian race. A professor in Göttingen, Johann Friedrich Blumenbach, invents the science of physiology, which ultimately becomes physical anthropology. Blumenbach divides the world into five races, but makes no value judgments, other than aesthetic ones, about them. White people have the "face which is normally regarded as the most beautiful and agreeable," and he decides to call them Caucasians, "because it is in that region that the finest race of men is to be found, the Georgian race." It is Blumenbach's theory that Georgia was the birthplace of mankind and that all the other races derive from the Georgians, with their "beautifully shaped skulls."

[Johann Gottfried von Herder, 1784: "The Negro has as much right to term his savage robbers albinos and white devils as we have to deem him the emblem of evil, and a descendant of Ham, branded by his father's curse."]

Races: For the taxonomist Carolus Linnaeus in 1793, the order *Anthropomorpha* has four varieties: *Eurapaeus albus* ("ingenious, inventive, sanguineous . . . governed by law"); *Americanus rubesceus* ("happy with his lot, freedom-loving, irascible . . . governed by custom"); *Asiaticus luridus* ("proud, avaricious, melancholy . . . governed by opinion"); and *Afer niger* ("crafty, lazy, careless, apathetic . . . governed by the arbitrary will of his masters").

In 1805, Johan Christian Fabricius, who believes that blacks are the result of interbreeding between whites and apes, discovers that there are two kinds of lice, quite different in color and shape: a human louse (*pediculus humanus*) and a Negro louse *(pediculus nigritarum).*

F. W. Schelling in 1806 divides humanity into "two great masses," in which "the human element seems only to exist in one of its halves." "Only the ancestor of that race which was ready to endure all, the Japhetic, Promethean, Caucasian race could be the Unique Man capable by his own act of breaking through into the world of Ideas."

For the philosopher Christoph Meiners (who would be celebrated by the Nazis) in 1811, there are again only two races: one fair and beautiful, the other dark and ugly. Within these divisions, however, there are innumerable gradations from bestiality to heroic civilization.

Whereas people, and even races, had once been classified and stereotyped according to languages or geography or religion or technological accomplishment, physiology now provides a scientific method of measurement, description, and comparison, one which happens to reinforce existing, previously unscientific beliefs about ethnic differences. Physiology is most enthusiastically endorsed in Germany, where it was born; in America, with its large slave population; and in France, which has been shaken by the slave revolt in Haiti in the 1790's and the rise of Toussaint L'Ouverture. Saint-Simon in 1803: "The revolutionaries applied the principle of equality to negroes. Had they consulted the physiologists they would have learned that the negro is organically incapable, in a situation where he can obtain the same teaching, of being educated to the same level of intelligence as the European."

Origin is destiny: an idea that never dies. In 1824, the French romantic historian, Augustin Thierry, writes: "Recent studies in physiology. . . show that the physical and moral constitution of nations depends on their descent from certain primitive ancestors."

In England, however, in the first half of the 19th century, Reason and Science have not yet replaced the Word of God, and their colonies, moreover, remain relatively peaceful. The leading British ethnologist is James Cowles Pritchard, who founds the Ethnological Society of London, devoted to tying "all men together into a single ethnological family tree," by using "the comparison of languages to establish affinities between physically dissimilar groups." Following the system proposed by Jacob Bryant in 1774 in an *Analysis of Antient Mythology,* he subscribes to the classification of peoples according to the sons of Noah, but whereas Bryant had argued that climate caused some of the Hamites to become dark-skinned, Pritchard believes the opposite. Adam and Eve were black, and it is the effects of civilization that causes the skin to become lighter. In France, America, and Germany, race determines civilization; in England, civilization determines race.

4.

In 1773, the Honourable East India Company commissions eleven pandits in the city of Calcutta to compile a digest of Hindu law. Their book, *The Bridge Across the Ocean of Litigation*, is translated from Sanskrit into Persian by Zayn al-Din Ali Rasa'i, and then from Persian into English by Nathaniel Brassey Halhed. Published in 1776 as *The Code of Gentoo Laws*, Halhed's introduction contains the surprising information that "Shanscrit" is "the Parent of almost every dialect from the Persian Gulph to the China Seas," and that the Maharajah of Krishnagar has in his possession ancient books that not only give an account of communication between India and Egypt—then considered the oldest advanced civilization—but also describe the Egyptians as disciples of the Indians.

In 1783, William Jones arrives in Calcutta. Already well known as a prodigy and a translator from the Persian, Arabic, and Turkish, but penurious in his position as a tutor to an aristocratic family, he had successfully applied for a judgeship, hoping to earn enough money to retire to a country estate and a life of independent scholarship. In India, he forms the Asiatick Society, whose *Journal*, thanks to Jones' fame and rising Indophilia, becomes immensely popular, going through countless authorized and pirated editions in English, and in French and German translation.

In 1786, in his third Anniversary Discourse to the Society, in a paragraph that becomes a sensation, Jones extends Halhed's claims for Sanskrit and announces his discovery of an Indo-European *ur*-language:

The *Sanscrit* language, whatever be its antiquity, is of a wonderful structure; more perfect than the *Greek*, more copious than the *Latin*, and more exquisitely refined than either, yet bearing to both of them a stronger affinity, both in the roots of verbs and in the forms of grammar, than could possibly have been produced by accident; so strong indeed, that no philologer could examine them all three, without believing them to have sprung from some common source, which, perhaps, no longer exists: there is a similar reason, though not quite so forcible, for supposing that both the *Gothick* and the *Celtick*, though blended with a very different idiom, had the same origin with the *Sanscrit*; and the old *Persian* might be added to the same family, if this were the place for discussing any question concerning the antiquities of *Persia*.

[Jones' famous discovery had already been made in obscurity in 1767 by an Irish scholar, James Parsons, in a book appropriately titled *The Remains of Japheth, being historical enquiries into the affinity and origins of the European languages*.]

In his nine discourses, Jones attempts to reconcile his linguistic discoveries with Genesis. As the descendants of the three sons of Noah, he assigns the Indians, Egyptians, Greeks, Romans, Goths, Chinese, Japanese, Tibetans, Southeast Asians, Incas, and Aztecs to Ham; the Arabs, Jews, Assyrians, and Abyssinians to Shem; and the Tartars and nearly all nomadic groups in Asia and the Americas to Japheth. He states that there are not only linguistic similarities within each lineage, but also similar religions and degrees of accomplishment in the arts and technology. (He admits, however, that a comparison of the languages from the three groups shows no common words among them; thus it is impossible to recover the Original Language, spoken by Adam, before Babel.) At least one reviewer questions the inexplicable absence of black Africans from this scheme, and wonders why the cursed prog-

eny of Ham have become the rulers of the world: "The male-
diction of the Patriarch seems to have operated in a manner
diametrically opposite to His wishes." This inversion may be
a product of Jones' egalitarianism: In England, he had written
a controversial pamphlet calling for universal education; in
his first address to the Asiatick Society, he had called for the
admission of Indian scholars.

India has now joined Egypt, Greece, or the Holy Land—
depending on the authority—as the primary repository of
ancient knowledge, either as the very foundation of Western
civilization or as part of a forgotten network of influence.

John Zephaniah Holwell, claiming that India had instructed the Egyptians, Hebrews, and Greeks, presents a translation
of Hindu scriptures (whose originals have never been found)
which rewrite and explain all the "incomprehensible difficul-
ties" in the Bible.

Various authors promote Hinduism as a monotheistic religion, revealed before the Hebrew version, that had degenerated in recent centuries into superstitious idolatry.

Lord Monboddo, contrary to Howell, states that the first
civilization was Egyptian, which was spread by Osiris himself
to Greece and India. The language of Greece had originally
been Egyptian, but had changed over the centuries. In India,
however, it had been preserved by conservative Brahmins;
thus Sanskrit was unadulterated ancient Egyptian.

Capt. Francis Wilford, in his translation of the *Puranas*,
demonstrates that they contain the same stories as the Bible,
Greek and Egyptian mythology, and the names of places as far
away as Britain. (Some years later, he discovers that the texts
he was working from, copied out by a pandit in his employ,
include some 12,000 additional verses that had been invented
by the pandit to please his employer and inspire further commissions.)

The Irish patriot Charles Vallancey, who believes that
Irish is the oldest language in the world, traces of which can
be found from Algonquin to Japanese, finds confirmation of
his theories in India. In 1786, he publishes *A Vindication of the
Ancient History of Ireland*. (William Jones comments: "Do you

wish to laugh? Skim the book over. Do you wish to sleep?
Read it regularly.") In 1797, he expands his thesis to *The
Ancient History of Ireland, Proved from the Sanscrit Books of the
Bramins of India.*

5.

In 1802, Alexander Hamilton—one of two people in Europe
with a thorough knowledge of Sanskrit—goes to Paris during
a short-lived peace, and is made a prisoner of war when hos-
tilities resume. It is, however, a strange captivity, as he is
allowed to live where he pleases, help catalog the Indian manuscripts in the Bibliothèque Nationale, and give classes in
Sanskrit to a few students. Among them are Friedrich von
Schlegel, the first to translate directly from Sanskrit into
German, and his brother August Wilhelm, who becomes the
first German professor of Sanskrit. (A third brother, Carl
August—the only one of the three to go to India—had died in
Madras as an officer of the East India Company in 1789.)

F. von Schlegel believes that Indian mythology and poetry
will be an inspiration for the "brutal and dull" culture of
Germany—a view more or less shared by all the lights of
German Romanticism—and moreover that "everything,
absolutely everything, has its origin in India." Civilization
was born in the foothills of the Himalayas, but some ancient
crime turned the gentle vegetarians into carnivores and set
them out into the world. Indians had taught the Egyptians,
who in turn had founded a colony in Judea, where Indian wisdom was only partially taught to the Jews. (Moses refused to
tell them about metempsychosis or the immortality of the
soul, for these had already fallen into gross superstition.) And
they had traveled as far as northern Europe in search of a
magic mountain that, in their mythology, was to be found
somewhere in the North—for India, of course, had a "supernatural idea of the high dignity and splendor of the North."

In his *On the Language and Wisdom of the Indians* (1808), F. von
Schlegel writes that Sanskrit, the "antediluvian language," is

perfect. All languages may be divided into two groups: inflected (where the root word becomes internally modified) and agglutinative (where particles are affixed to the word). Inflected languages—such as Sanskrit and German—are as natural as plants, divinely created, living organisms that stimulate intelligence. Agglutinative languages—such as Hebrew and Chinese—are "mere conglomerations of atoms." [These linguistic stereotypes have, however, no overt political agenda. Though often considered the father of modern anti-Semitism, Schlegel was married to the daughter of the philosopher Moses Mendelssohn and advocated Jewish rights.]

Among A. W. von Schlegel's students is Franz Bopp, who, in 1816, with the publication of his *Conjugationssystem der Sanskrit*, turns the discovery of the relationship between Sanskrit and Greek and Latin into a new science, comparative philology. This, in turn, joins with physiology to form a new discipline, called "comparative philology and ethnology," a system of classifying cultures first by language, then by physical type, and then by social traits. It is decades before the two split apart.

What to call the new *ur*-language? Thomas Young, an Englishman, in 1816 coins the word "Indo-European." F. von Schlegel in 1819 calls it "Aryan," taking a term in Herodotus, *Arioi*, which had been adopted by Anquetil du Peyron, to designate the Persians and Medes, because he hears a coincidence between the root *ari* and the German *Ehre*, meaning "honor." Julius von Klaproth counters Young in 1823 with "Indo-Germanic," which most of the German scholars (except Bopp, who prefers "Indo-Classical") adopt. In 1851, Boetticher-Lagarde calls it the "Japhetic" language.

The translation of the single word "yoga" in A. W. von Schlegel's 1823 Latin version of the *Bhagavad-Gita* sets off an international polemic on the translatability of cultures, and a general meditation on the relation between language and culture. Schlegel had chosen numerous words to render "yoga," according to the context: *destinatio, exercitatio, applicatio, devotio, disciplina activa, facultas mystica, maiestas, mysterium, contemplatio*. From France, his most virulent critic, A. S. Langlois, insists that it should be translated as a single word: the French *dévotion*. Schlegel replies that one cannot treat the "poetic representation of the mind's innermost conceptions of itself and the eternal" like a collection of algebraic signs. (To put it another way: translation has no =.) Wilhelm von Humboldt, a minister of state for Prussia and a leading Sanskritist, declares that both approaches are possible, but that the word essentially cannot be translated because "a people's speech is their spirit and the spirit is their speech." Each language represents, more than its sounds and signs, a different worldview. Although unintentional on Humboldt's part, this theory will chime perfectly with the classification systems of comparative philology and ethnology, and its resultant racial characterizations.

A.W. von Schlegel, 1804: "If the regeneration of the human species started in the East, then Germany must be considered the Orient of Europe."

F. Schelling, 1805: "What is Europe really but a sterile trunk which owes everything to oriental grafts?"

In 1812, Othmar Frank calls for a "Society for the Ancient Wisdom of the Orient and of the German Nation."

In 1820, the geographer Karl Ritter describes Buddhist armies crossing the Caucasus westward.

Michelet, 1827: "India is the womb of the world. . . . From India descends a torrent of light, a river of Law and Reason."

In 1828, Wilhelm von Humboldt thanks God for allowing him to live long enough to read the *Bhagavad-Gita*.

By the 1830's, German schoolchildren are studying Sanskrit.

Pierre Leroux, 1832: "Why should we now restrict ourselves to the Jewish Pantheon when we have been illuminated by this light which has begun to spread right across the horizon?"

Balzac, 1833: "The history of the origin of man in the Bible is only the genealogy of a swarm which came out of the human hive hanging on the mountainsides of Tibet between the summits of Himalaya and the Caucasus. . . . A great history rests beneath these names and places, behind these fictions which attract us irresistibly without our knowing why. Perhaps we breathe in them the air of our new humanity."

In 1845, Christian Lassen writes that the Indo-Germans are the most superior of the Caucasians (among which he includes the Semites): "the most highly organized, the most enterprising, and the most creative among the peoples."

In 1848, in a popular book, Jacob Grimm tells the tale of a people "propelled from East to West by an irresistible instinct": "The vocation and courage of those people. . . is shown by the fact that European history was almost entirely made by them." He calls them, not Aryans or Indo-Germans, but simply the *Deutschen*, and he includes among them the Franks, Burgundians, and Lombards.

Lamartine, 1853: "India is the key to everything."

6.

Hamilton taught Schlegel; Schlegel taught Bopp; Bopp taught Friedrich Max Müller, the most famous Sanskritist of the 19th century and the tireless propagandist for the Aryan race. Max Müller arrives in Oxford in 1846 to translate the *Rig Veda* ("the first book of the Aryan nation") and remains until his death in 1900, never having visited India. His translation has been commissioned by the East India Company for the unfathomable sum of £10,000—which they never paid—thanks to the promotions of Thomas Babbington Macaulay, who, while serving on the Company's Supreme Council, had called for universal education in India as a way to eradicate idolatry. It is Macaulay's belief that a serious study of the Vedic texts by the Indians will reveal the errors of their ways and hasten their conversion to Christianity. Max Müller himself writes that the Vedas are "the root of their religion and to show them what the root is, I feel sure, is the only way of uprooting all that has sprung from it during the last three thousand years."

By this time, it has been discovered that there are three linguistic families on the subcontinent: the so-called Indo-Aryan (to which Sanskrit belongs) in the north, the Dravidian in the south, and the Munda or Austro-Asiatic, spoken by various tribal peoples, mainly in the east. It is thought by some that Dravidian is a Semitic language, and therefore its speakers are among the Children of Shem. Sanskrit is not, as was once believed, the original pan-Indian language.

In the *Rig Veda*, the gods, the Children of Arya who "seek and are led by light," battle and conquer dark-skinned demons, the Dasyus or Dasas, the forces of darkness, and thereby obtain fire, dawn, the sun, and the day. Max Müller reads this cosmic battle—almost universal in mythology—as the literal history of an invasion of India.

The earliest known manuscripts of the *Rig Veda* come from around 300 B.C.E.. Max Müller, fitting his history into Bishop Ussher's Biblical chronology, claims that this Aryan invasion took place around 1500 B.C.E. (eight hundred years after the Flood) and that the *Rig Veda* was composed around 1200 B.C.E. and preserved intact orally by the Brahmins for a thousand years. Because Indo-Aryan languages are spoken in the north, because the Vedas were written in Sanskrit, and because of historically known conquests of northern India, Max Müller assumes that Sanskrit was the language of these invaders.

In 1847, he sets out his theory: There are two races in India: the older, Dravidian-speaking race, which he considers Cushite or Hamite or Negro, and the Indo-Germanic or Caucasian or Japhetite or Aryan race, which conquered part, but not all, of the country. The northern Indians are civilized Caucasians whose skin simply darkened from the sun; they are not black savages, and have not, as is commonly believed, degenerated into savagery by mingling with the darker race. "We generally find that is the fate of the negro race, when brought into hostile contact with the Japhetic race, to be either destroyed or annihilated, or to fall into a state of slavery and degradation, from which, if at all, it recovers by the slow process of assimilation." In Oxford he declares that it is now the task of the descendants of the Indo-Germans—the British—"to accomplish the glorious work of civilization, which had been left unfinished by their Aryan brethren."

In one of his most stirring evocations of the Aryan theory, Max Müller writes:

> As sure as the six Romance dialects point to an original home of Italian shepherds on the seven hills of Rome, the Aryan languages together point to an earlier period of language, when the first ancestors of the Indians, the Persians, the Greeks, the Romans, the Slavs, the Celts, and the Germans were living together within the same enclosures, nay, under the same roof. Before the ancestors of the Indians and the Persians started for the south, and the leaders of the Greek, Roman, Celtic, Teutonic, and Slavonic colonies marched towards the shores of Europe, there was a small clan of Aryans, settled probably on the highest elevation of Central Asia, speaking a language, not yet Sanskrit or Greek or German, but containing the dialectic germs of all; a clan that had advanced to the state of agricultural civilization; that had recognized the bonds of blood, and sanctioned the bonds of marriage; and that invoked the Giver of Light and Life in heaven by the same name which you may still hear in the temples of Benares, in the basilicas of Rome, and in our own churches and cathedrals.

This clan, he notes, was "separate from the ancestors of the Semitic and Turanian [all non-Semitic, non-Aryan, and non-African] races":

> They have been the prominent actors in the great drama of history. . . . They have perfected society and morals. . . . In the continual struggle with Semitic and Turanian races, these Aryan nations have become the rulers of history, and it seems to be their mission to link all parts of the world together by the chains of civilization, commerce, and religion.

The American Sanskritist W. D. Whitney laughs at the idea of the Aryan "perched for a couple of thousand years upon some exalted post of observation, watching thence the successive departure from their ancient home of the various European tribes" and wonders if perhaps Max Müller hasn't been looking at too many German Romantic paintings of the dispersion of the peoples after the destruction of the Tower of Babel. Indeed, it is to Max Müller's own lineage, as the son of the Romantic poet Wilhelm Müller, that one may attribute passages such as this:

> The fathers of the Aryan race, the fathers of our own
> race, gathered together in the great temple of nature,
> like brothers of the same house, and looked up in ado-
> ration to the sky as the emblem of what they yearned
> for, a father and a god.

7.

In 1853, Joseph Arthur de Gobineau, in what he calls a "means to assuage a hatred of democracy and of the Revolution," and in the belief that civilization is dying, invents a new mythology and a new science to explain it. According to his influential *Essay on the Inequality of the Human Races*, the races result from precise mixings of blood, a "historical chemistry" which may be measured. ("Hellenes: Aryans modified by yellow elements but with a great preponderance of the white essence and some Semitic affinities." "Aborigines: Slavo-Celtic peoples saturated with yellow elements." Etc.) Breeding between the races has a natural "law of repulsion." However, war and conquest produce a "law of attraction" that leads to miscegenation. There are only white people in Genesis. From their post-diluvian home somewhere in northern Asia, the Sons of Ham were the first to set out to conquer the world, became "saturated in black blood," and degenerated. (Gobineau avoids the question of where this black blood came from.) The next to set out were the Sons of Shem, the Semites, whose blood mixed to a lesser degree and thus were less degraded. The Sons of Japheth, the Aryans, remained pure until the

Christian era, but now they too were set on a course that
would lead to their ruin:

> The white species will disappear henceforth from the
> face of the earth. After passing through the age of the
> gods when it was absolutely pure; the age of heroes,
> in which the mixtures were moderate in strength and
> number; the age of the nobility, where human facul-
> ties remained considerable though they could not be
> renewed from dried-up sources, it has descended,
> more or less swiftly according to the environment, to
> a final confusion of all the elements. . . . The portion
> of Aryan blood, already subdivided so frequently,
> which still exists in our countries and which alone
> sustains the edifice of our society, advances daily
> toward the last frontier before total absorption. When
> this result is achieved. . . it will be the last stage of
> mediocrity in all its aspects; mediocrity in physical
> strength, mediocrity in beauty, mediocrity in intellec-
> tual aptitudes, one might almost say annihilation.

About three thousand years from now will be "the final spasm
of our species, when the lifeless earth will continue, without
us, to describe its apathetic orbits in space."

[In 1856, Ernst Renan writes to Gobineau: "You have written
a most remarkable book full of vigor and originality of mind,
only it is not at all written to be understood in France, or
rather it is written to be misunderstood. The French intelligence does not adapt itself easily to ethnographic considera-
tions."]

The Sanskrit word *arya* means "noble." *Arya* was attached to
proper names as an honorific, like "Sir." A woman addressed
her husband as "son of Arya." The Buddha called his teachings the Arya Dharma; Buddhism has an Arya Marga, the
path of nobility, and the *Dhammapada* states that "One who
destroys life is never an Arya, and one who desists from taking life is an Arya." In the *Ramayana*, the god Rama is

described as an "Arya who cared for the equality of all and was dear to everyone." In its thirty-six occurrences in the *Rig Veda*, *arya* is almost always an adjective: the Aryan laws govern the universe; a beautiful tree is Aryan. *Arya* is a human or superhuman quality, a standard of behavior, a state of cosmic order; there is no evidence in the texts that it refers to an ethnic or racial group. Those who follow the laws are Aryan; those who do not (including foreigners, non-Vedic indigenous groups, and wicked individuals) are Dasyu. However, thanks to the proselytizing of Max Müller and Gobineau, "Aryan," referring to a race, becomes a commonplace in the West and largely replaces "Japhetite" as a classification for white people who are not "Semites." The Indian component, with its physical differences that must be explained, recedes in importance. By 1903, Enrico de Michaelis would declare that India is no longer the cradle of civilization, but the grave of the Aryans.

8.

In the second half of the 19th century, with the discoveries of the geologists and paleontologists, the prevailing 6,000-year Biblical chronology is largely overthrown. (Although in England, P. H. Gosse, for one, claims that God created the world with geological strata and the fossilized remains of creatures that never existed.) India and Egypt are now known to be not the beginnings of human history, but relatively recent developments. The races are far older than the language groups, and therefore quite different people could easily speak the same language; philology no longer provides a narrative of mankind's origins. The disciplines of philology and ethnology split apart, and quarrel. [A leading text in the debate is A. F. Pott's 1856 *Essay on the Inequality of the Human Races*, which is subtitled *Especially from the Point of View of Philological Science*, and sub-subtitled: *Based on a Consideration of the Work of Count Gobineau which Bears the Same Title*.]

Around 1860, ethnology (anthropology) becomes institutionalized as a discipline, and its primary goal is to classify the different types of humans, mainly according to the new systems

of anthropometrics, under the rule of Paul Broca's fantastic
contraptions for measuring "cephalic indices" and other
markers. Paul Topinard's "nasal index," for example, divides
the human nose into three categories— leptorrhine (narrow),
platyrhine (broad), and mesorhine (medium)—corresponding
to the three races of man: white, black, yellow. (Topinard also
claims that the non-white races are incapable of counting
beyond 2, 3, or 5.) James Hunt demonstrates that the inferior-
ity of blacks is due to the fact that their cranial sutures close
earlier than that of whites, putting an osseous limit on their
mental growth. "Young Negro children are nearly as intelligent as European children," but after puberty their advancement comes to a halt. Cephalic indices are used to prove,
among other things, the inferior intellects of European women
("to a far greater extent than that of a Negress to a Negro")
and that the Chinese are incapable of understanding metaphysics.

For many decades, Gustav Klemm's *General History of
Civilization* is the standard German text on the subject. He
describes a kind of yin and yang of humanity, "male" and
"female" civilizations, active and passive, strong and weak,
intellectual and servile. The female races include not only
blacks, but Russians and Slavs: "The serfs display the signs of
their passive origins in their ample cheek-bones, their eyes
which are small and slanting, their thick flat noses, and their
dark or livid complexions."

In 1865, Marx enthusiastically recommends an account by a
French traveler, Pierre Trémaux, to Engels: "In practical and
historical application, Trémaux is far richer and more important than Darwin. Thus certain questions, such as nationality,
etc., he explains simply on a natural basis." Trémaux's central
thesis is that the geological nature of the soil determines the
race and characteristics of the people living on it. If Africans
moved to Europe they would turn white, and vice versa. For
Marx, who agrees with Klemm about the Russians and the
Slavs, this accounts for their barbarity. Engels, however, is
unimpressed: "How does this person explain why we

Rhinelanders on our secondary Devonian mountains have not long ago been turned into idiots or niggers?"

In 1871, Edward Burnett Tylor invents the scientific classification of "cultures" (a word he is the first to use in its currently accepted sense):

> The principle criteria of classification are the absence or presence, high or low development, of the industrial arts, the extent of scientific knowledge, the definiteness of moral principles, the condition of religious belief and ceremony, the degree of social and political organization, and so forth. Thus, on the definite basis of compared facts, ethnographers are able to set up at least a rough scale of civilization. Few would dispute that the following races are arranged rightly in order of culture: Australian, Tahitian, Aztec, Chinese, Italian.

Ethnology's emphasis is on differences and, combined with the new Darwinian and Spencerian ideas of natural selection and survival of the fittest, becomes a refutation of theological and politically utopian ideas of equality. Moreover, there is unrest in the British colonies: the 1857 Sepoy Rebellion forces the British government to rule India directly; in Jamaica eight years later, a protest by freed slaves is violently suppressed by the governor and many hundreds are executed. (His actions are not only supported by the predictable Thomas Carlyle—author of *Occasional Discourse Upon the Nigger Question*—but also by Ruskin, Tennyson, and, surprisingly, Dickens.) The British imperial mission, the "white man's burden," having found its scientific justification in evolution and physiology, also demands ancient historical validation. Pritchard's *The Eastern Origin of the Celtic Nations* is replaced by Isaac Taylor's *The Origins of the Aryans: An Account of the Prehistoric Ethnology and Civilization of Europe*. Taylor is not only Darwinian, but cautionary: A white-skinned people from the West conquered the dark-skinned savages of northern India and brought them civilization, but they intermarried with the locals, their skin darkened, and their society degenerated.

The mixing of the races: In 1890, the American anthropologist Daniel Garrison Brinton—who had given his translation of the Mayan *Popol Vuh* the title *Rig Vedas Americanus*—states that mulattoes are "deficient in physical vigor," and that "the third generation of descendants of a marriage between the white and the Polynesian, Australian, or Dravidian, become extinct through short lives, feeble constitutions, or sterility." White women have "no holier duty, no more sacred mission, than that of transmitting in its integrity the heritage of ethnic endowment gained by the race through thousands of generations of struggle."

In 1896, Frederick L. Hoffman, measuring the heels of Negroes, mulattoes, and whites, proves that "when a race of a lower degree of civilization comes in contact with a superior race," the result is that the inferior race takes on some of the external, "ornamental" characteristics of the superior race— the feet of mulattoes are smaller than those of Negroes—but their "vital and moral characteristics" are even more inferior.

9.

In 1851, Schopenhauer had defined the mission: "We may hope that Europe will free itself some day of all Jewish mythology. Perhaps the century is approaching when the peoples of the Japhetic stock, originating in Asia, will find the sacred relics of their native land, because, after having gone astray for so long, they have reached sufficient maturity for this." Aryanism becomes a unifying force in Germany, a new sense of "us" that transcends the political factions. When unification is finally achieved in 1871, Sir Henry Maine declares: "a nation has been born out of Sanskrit."

With the Franco-Prussian War (1870–71), the German-Aryan nationalist agenda clashes with French claims for its share of the Ancient Wisdom and sets off a debate, waged with craniometers, over who are the true Aryans. Armand de Quatrefuges, the head of the French school of anthropology, having witnessed the brutal bombardment of Paris, writes that the Germans are not Aryans at all, but must be Finns, or worse, Slavo-Finns, barbarians who go back to the days when Europe had rhinoceroses and elephants. The theory is extremely popular in France, and the Germans respond by initiating a ten-year project of measuring the skulls of fifteen million schoolchildren in various countries. The study proves, for its investigators, that there are two types in Europe: the dark and brachycephalic (round-headed), who are considered to be aboriginals, and the blond and dolichocephalic (long-headed) Aryans who conquered them. To close the case, an investigative committee goes to Finland and proves that, contrary to popular belief, Finns are blond, and therefore Aryan.

French and Italian scientists object, and produce alternate investigations and conclusions: that dark brachys are the true Aryans; or that the French were originally dolicho-blond Aryans but had been diluted by dark brachys; or that it was the French who Aryanized the Germans; or that the Germans are degenerated Hindu and Persian Aryans; or . . .

Meanwhile, "Ammon's Law," developed by Otto Ammon, states that urban populations are more dolichocephalic because dolichocephalics show "a stronger inclination to city life and a greater aptitude for success there." (Asked to provide a photograph of a "pure Alpine type," Ammon replies that he cannot, as he has not yet found a perfect specimen.) Charles Closson elaborately refines this law, even down to the "greater taxpaying capacity of the dolichocephalic population."

In 1899, a dolicho-blond French chauvinist, Count Georges Vacher de Lapouge—whose assistant measuring skulls had been the young Paul Valéry, future creator of Monsieur Teste— amidst his scientific proofs that the Germans lived like monkeys while the French were cultivating wheat, makes this prophecy:

> The conflict of nations is now about to start openly within nations and between nations. . . . I am convinced that in the next century people will slaughter each other by the million because of a difference of a

degree or two in the cephalic index. It is by this sign
. . . that men will be identified . . . and the last senti-
mentalists will be able to witness the most massive
exterminations of peoples.

10.

Aryanism, a self-celebration of the German people through
the revival of folk dances and costumes and tales, and an
intellectual linkage to the Ancient Wisdom of India, transcends political differences and leads to the unification of the
country. With the rise of the Second Reich, sudden industrial-
ization (decades behind France and England), and large
migrations (especially by Jews) into the cities, it turns into a
Romantic nostalgia for the forests, for clean living, and a small
homogeneous population. It creates a cult of the body: nud-
ism, vegetarianism (which Hitler would later practice), and
sexual liberation (which would unite nationalists and
bohemians). Judeo-Christianity, the religion of the Children of
Shem, becomes the enemy of the Japhetite, Aryan religion.
Rituals are revived or invented: sun-worship (first celebrated
by Max Müller as the original Aryan religion), altars to the old
Teutonic gods, the casting of magic runes, seances where one
can speak to the ancestors, even pseudo-Vedic horse sacrifices.
Those aspects of Indian culture that will serve—most notably
the caste system—are selected as proof of ancient Aryan ways.

Madame Blavatsky—after her move to India in 1878—and
Nietzsche simultaneously fixate on the Indian caste of pari-
ahs, the *chandalas*. Blavatsky, in her incomprehensibly complex cyclical history of the world in *The Secret Doctrine*, reveals
that we are now in the moment of the ascendancy of the fifth
Aryan sub-race, the Teutonic, known for its scientific accomplishment and soon to attain spiritual advancement. The Jews
are the "expelled *chandala* of Ancient India," who wandered to
Egypt, and are "materially degenerate in intellect." "The
Semitic languages are the bastard descendants of the first corruption of the eldest children of early Sanskrit." Nietzsche on
the Hindu *Laws of Manu*:

These orders are instructive enough—in them we have on the one hand Aryan humanity, completely pure, completely original—we learn that the idea of "pure blood" is the opposite of a harmless concept. On the other hand, it becomes clear which people perpetuated a hatred, a *chandala* hatred, against this humanity, which became a religion and a genius. . . . Christianity, from a Jewish root and only understandable as a plant from this soil, represents the counter movement to every moral of breeding, race, and privilege—it is the anti-Aryan religion par excellence; Christianity overhauls all Aryan values, the victory of the *chandala* values—the Gospel preached to the poor and low, the collected revolt of all the down-trodden, the miserable, the failed, those who have come off poorly in the race—the immortal *chandala* revenge as a religion of love.

Heinrich Schliemann, in his spectacular excavation of Troy in the 1870's, finds hundreds of artifacts marked with swastikas. Believing that the Trojans were related to the Teutons, noting the presence of the swastika in other Aryan cultures from India to Ireland (and ignoring its presence in practically all other cultures), he declares that it is the most "significant religious symbol of our ancestors." He decorates his mansion in Athens—where his wife entertains wearing Helen's supposed diadem—with a large band of swastikas running around its outside walls. Schliemann's fame sets off an international swastika mania, much of it benign: the swastika as "earliest known symbol" (according to the title of a monograph published by the Smithsonian Institution in 1896) or as the preeminent Aryan insignia or simply as a good luck charm. Swastikas appear on advertisements, cigar bands, deodorants, Boy Scout badges, and American high school yearbooks as good luck charms, on the spines of Kipling's books as a bridge between India and England and on Yeats' books as a sign of Indo-Celtic spirituality, and on the emblems of Madame Blavatsky's Theosophical Society, and other, more sinister occultist, militarist, and pan-Germanic groups, before it is taken over by the German National Socialists.

The century begins with the massive and erudite *Foundations of the Nineteenth Century* by Houston Stewart Chamberlain, Wagner's son-in-law, which becomes a bestseller in Germany and abroad, praised by Wilhelm II, Bernard Shaw, and Teddy Roosevelt, among others. The intellectual handbook of Aryanism, it is a detailed history of the Manichean struggle between the only two pure races left on earth, the Teutons and the Jews (the rest are a "chaos of peoples"); one, the creator of all things good in Western civilization; the other, the destroyer, with no imagination or ideals, only an iron will to power. Even Christianity, a Persian religion founded by Jesus (who "had not a drop of genuinely Jewish blood in his veins") and based on the "sacred 'Three in Number' of the Aryans," had been perverted into exalting a single God, first by St. Paul, a Jew, and then by Ignatius Loyola, a non-Aryan Basque. [Similarly, Madame Blavatsky, had claimed that the Kabbalah was an Aryan mystical practice usurped by the Jews.] Where the Romantics had portrayed the ancient Germans as disciples of Greece and Rome—philosophers in the forest— Chamberlain states that all the glories of the classical world were the products of German influence or even German leaders.

After Einstein announces the theory of relativity, Chamberlain crusades against "Jewish physics," with its "all-powerful arbitrariness," in contrast to "Aryan physics," based on a three-dimensional and logical universe. In 1927, as Chamberlain lay dying, Hitler would come to kiss his hands.

Around 1912, the new science of psychoanalysis splits into Freudian-Jewish and Jungian-Aryan branches. Jung, however, is after more than helping the mentally ill: He imagines the creation of a new religion that would strip away the millennia of Judeo-Christianity and liberate the inner Aryan ancestor. His "collective unconscious" becomes a vast compendium and synthesis of the gods, rites, symbols, and motifs that writers from the scholarly to the occult to the kitsch have attributed to the Aryans for the last fifty years.

[In the Jung circle that would eventually be associated with the Bollingen Foundation and the Eranos Seminars, many of the best scholars are Aryanists who would become actively or passively Fascist, combining the Aryan rejection of Judeo-Christianity, interest in folk culture, and the elaboration of archaic connections among cultures. Mircea Eliade, propagandist for the Romanian Fascist group, the Iron Guard. Georges Dumézil, prewar Nazi sympathizer and postwar ultrarightist. Giuseppe Tucci, the century's major Tibetologist who, during the war, would wear Fascist uniforms at official functions and edit a magazine devoted to fostering cultural ties between Italy and Japan. Agehananda Bharati, expert on Tantrism, born Leopold Fischer and a Nazi. Henri Corbin, favorite of the Pahlevi court and promoter of a Prusso-Persian Aryanism. D. T. Suzuki, the primary purveyor of Zen in the West and militant Japanese nationalist. Eugen Herrigel, author of *Zen in the Art of Archery* and a Nazi.]

While Jung is claiming that Freudian analysis is applicable only to Jews, Sándor Ferenczi is writing to Freud: "It struck me that in the Zurich mental hospitals dementia praecox [schizophrenia] was so much more prevalent than in Hungarian ones. This illness is evidently the natural condition, as it were, of Nordic man, who has not yet completely overcome the last period of the Ice Age."

In 1917, the United States, alarmed by the "yellow peril" of the arriving Chinese and Japanese, passes an immigration law allowing only "free white" people to enter the country permanently. In 1923, a Brahmin from the Punjab sues for citizenship on the grounds that he is a member of the Aryan race. The case goes to the Supreme Court, which rules against him, stating that intermarriage has destroyed "the purity of Aryan blood" and that "the average man knows perfectly well that there are unmistakable and profound differences" between "the blond Scandinavian and the brown Hindu."

In the 1920's, the discoveries of the great cities of the Indus Valley civilization, Harappa and Mohenjo-daro, prove that there was an advanced civilization on the subcontinent long before the Aryans arrived: beginning around 5500 B.C.E., flourishing from 2600 to 1900 B.C.E., covering an area twice the size of ancient Egypt or Mesopotamia, with some fifteen hundred towns and cities, whose artifacts, now that they are recognized as such, are found all over the Old World. The discovery is immediately placed in the existing historical narrative: The Indus Valley civilization collapsed when its cities were sacked by the invading Aryans and abandoned.

In the 1920's, after the German defeat and the national humiliation of the Versailles Treaty, the Aryan groups become increasingly obsessed with purification: moral rectitude, abstinence from alcohol and tobacco, eugenics, physical exercise, campaigns against prostitution and syphilis, and the elimination of Jews from all levels of society. The pagan, erotic, folkloric, anti-bourgeois elements are gradually purged and replaced by militarism. One of the largest Aryan groups, the Pan-Germanic Society, distributes free copies of the works of Gobineau; one third of its membership is schoolteachers, carrying the word to their classrooms.

Hitler, 1925:

> All human culture, all the results of art, science, and technology that we see before us today, are almost exclusively the creative product of the Aryan. He alone was the founder of all higher humanity, therefore representing the prototype of all that we understand by the word "man." He is the Prometheus of mankind from whose bright forehead the divine spark of genius has sprung at all times, forever kindling anew that fire of knowledge which illumined the night of silent mysteries and thus caused man to climb the path to mastery over the other beings of this earth. Exclude him—and perhaps after a few thousand years darkness will again descend on the earth, human culture will pass, and the world turn to a desert.

11.

At the other end of the Aryan world, parallel developments: In prison for thirteen years as an anti-British terrorist, V. D. Savarkar writes the manifesto of Hindu nationalism, *Hindutva* [*Hinduness*, 1923], an evocation of the common blood and Holy Land of Indo-Aryan greatness—perverted not by Jews, but by Muslims—written in the neo-Romantic style of Max Müller. *Hindutva* leads to the founding of the RSS, the National Volunteer Union. The RSS, with its military uniforms and celibate officers, promotes Hindu consciousness, moral rectitude, intolerance, and athletic prowess, through gymnastics, religious study, weapons training, elaborately staged demonstrations, and disruptions of Muslim festivals, all under a flag that features a swastika, a lotus, and a sword.

By 1930, the RSS and other similar groups realize they have much in common with German Fascism:

> Germany's solemn idea of the revival of Aryan culture, the glorification of the Swastika, her patronage of Vedic learning and the ardent championship of the tradition of Indo-Germanic civilization are welcomed by the religious and sensible Hindūs of India with a jubilant hope. Germany's crusade against the enemies of Aryan culture will bring all the Aryan nations of the world to their senses and awaken the Indian Hindus for the restoration of their lost glory.

Some even promote Hitler as an avatar of Vishnu. In Germany, however, the National Socialists split on the question of supporting Indian independence. One faction writes:

> For us, approval of the Indian fight for freedom from English domination and capitalist exploitation has been and is a necessity, as much from the fact that for a German liberation politics every weakening of a Versailles signatory is favorable, as from the emotional support of every battle which subjugated peoples enjoin against their exploitative usurpers, since it is a

compelling consequence of nationalism that the right
to fulfill a Volkish identity, which we claim for ourselves, also applies to other peoples and nations.

Hitler is unimpressed:

> An alliance of the downtrodden nations is a dumb slo-
> gan. . . . When today the Indian lives under the rule of
> England or the Black under the rule of any European
> people, this is grounded in their inferiority. The freedom
> fight of the Blacks, Indians, and so forth is an attempt to
> break the natural order . . . a racial perversity.

And his ideologue, Alfred Rosenberg—who believed that the
Aryans first came to India from Atlantis—elaborates:

> We know that the Hindus are a people in India who
> have been mixed from the high-ranking Aryan immi-
> grants and the dark-black original inhabitants and
> that this people today bears the consequences; for
> they are also the slaves of a race, and they appear to
> us in many respects almost like a second form of Jew.

With the advent of war, the Hindu nationalists split on the
question of supporting Germany. On the one hand, there is
Nazi racism; on the other, the common enemy, Britain. Some
develop a policy of temporarily supporting Britain until after
the war; others create clandestine German solidarity groups.
The Bengali nationalist Subhas Chandra Bose recruits among
the Indian prisoners of war in German camps and forms the
Indian Legionnaires, who march in uniforms decked with
Aryan eagles and swastikas, and are kept in ready by the
German High Command for the prospective invasions of
Afghanistan and the North-West Provinces that would become
Pakistan.

In 1948, Gandhi, the Hindu saint, is assassinated by a close
associate of Savarkar, the author of Hindu nationalism.

12.

At this moment, the standard histories tell the story of a mass migration of people from northern or western Asia, who traveled on their horse-drawn chariots west into Europe and, between 1500 and 1200 B.C.E., east into India, destroying the Indus Valley cities, and moving on to the Gangetic plain. There, they conquered the dark-skinned Dravidian-speaking peoples, imposed their Indo-European language, and instituted the caste system and a new "Vedic" religion, whose principal ritual was the horse sacrifice. The history of that invasion, and the beliefs and practices of that religion, are to be found in the *Rig Veda*, which was composed around 1200 B.C.E. and preserved orally for a thousand years until it was written down. Because of its association with Nazism, the term "Aryan" has been largely replaced (outside of India) by "Indo-European" as the name for these people.

At this moment, there is no archeological evidence for the existence of the Aryans, or of any mass migrations of people, or of a violent destruction of the Indus Valley cities, or of a widespread use of chariots (which would, in any event, have been unable to cross the mountains of the Hindu Kush), or of the horse sacrifice, or of anything at all mentioned in the *Rig Veda*, whose geographical features cannot even be identified in India. The historical fact of the Aryan invasion and the oral composition of the Vedas are entirely based on Max Müller's 1847 theories, as are its chronologies, which Max Müller had coordinated with the Biblical creation of the world.

Some now believe that the spread of the Indo-European languages occurred in remote antiquity, perhaps by conquest or migration before the Indus Valley civilization, perhaps during the flourishing of the Indus Valley through trade; and that the Indus Valley spoke a form of the language that later evolved into Sanskrit. Some believe that the *Rig Veda* is not ancient, that it was composed around 500 B.C.E., and was part of the contemporary religious upheavals that created Buddhism, Jainism, and modern Hinduism. The Vedic religion was a sect, devoted to the horse sacrifice and patriarchal gods, that was a failure and quickly vanished.

In India at this moment, prehistory is a contentious political issue. The Hindu nationalists maintain that there was no Aryan invasion, that the Vedas date from the third millennium B.C.E., that the religion of the Indus Valley was Vedic, and that the Indo-European languages, as the German Romantics believed, had their origins in India. Thus Hinduism—naturally evolving from a combination of the Vedic religion of the north and traditional beliefs in the south—and the Sanskrit-related languages are indigenous to India. Those who oppose the Hindu nationalists affirm the Aryan invasion history in all its details. Hinduism, like Islam, is a foreign religion imposed by conquest on the Indian peoples, and therefore India is no more intrinsically Hindu than it is Muslim. India is ruled by the Bhasratiya Janata Party, a descendant of the RSS that rose to power by destroying mosques, fomenting anti-Muslim riots, and rewriting laws and the names of cities to make them more authentically "Hindu." The ruins of Mohenjo-daro lie almost exactly halfway between Pokharan in the Thar Desert, where India exploded its atomic bomb, and the unnamed site in the Chagai Hills, where Pakistan exploded its own.

In the United States at this moment, there are periodic acts of violence committed in the name of Aryanism. Among the public groups and organizations that one may join are the Aryan Angels, the Aryan Corps, the Aryan Liberation Army, the Aryan Nations, the Aryan National Socialist Party, the Aryan Preservation Party, Aryan Uprising, White Aryan Resistance, and the Women for Aryan Unity. On the Internet, one may consult the Aryan Crusaders Library, the Aryan Female Homestead, the Aryan News Agency, the Pan-Aryan Resource Center, and innumerable chat groups and bulletin boards. There is an Aryan Dating Page, which is not a joke. The clicker at the home page for the Aryan Nations is now at twelve million visitors.

In the United States at this moment, certain states have passed laws that either actively discourage the teaching of evolution in public school or require that it be taught alongside "creationism" (or "creation science" as its proponents call it).

Creationism adheres to the Biblical narrative, but it has added—it is unclear how—four thousand years to Bishop Ussher's chronology; the world is now ten, not six, thousand years old. In certain states, biology textbooks are required to have stickers that read: "Evolution is a controversial theory some scientists present as a scientific explanation for the origin of living things. No one was present when life first appeared on earth. Therefore, any statement about life's origins should be considered as theory, not fact."

In 1795, Johann Friedrich Blumenbach had noted: "There seems to be so great a difference between widely separate nations. . . yet when the matter is thoroughly considered, you see that all do so run into one another, and that one variety of mankind does so sensibly pass into another, that you cannot mark out the limits between them."

In 1917, in an influential article in the *Journal of Delinquency*, Princeton lecturer Henry Goddard proved that, on the basis of IQ tests, 83% of immigrant Jews were "feeble-minded morons." Jews were slightly more intelligent, however, than American Indians, Mexicans, and Negroes. (Goddard coined the word "moron," and Margaret Sanger used his results as an argument for birth control.)

In 1921, Harvard professor Robert Yerkes proved that, on the basis of IQ tests administered to 1.75 million American soldiers, 37% of whites and 89% of Negroes were morons. The white average was so shockingly high because of the large numbers of immigrants from eastern and southern Europe. Italians, for example, had a mental age of 11.01; Poles, 10.74.

In 1923, Princeton professor C. C. Brigham popularized Yerkes' findings in a bestselling book, *A Study of American Intelligence*. Combining the IQ tests with craniometric evidence gathered by Count Vacher de Lapouge, Brigham proved that the United States was receiving the poorest specimens of European stock. Even worse, "the decline of American intelligence will be more rapid than the decline of the intelligence of European national groups, owing to the presence here of the negro." He recommended that "public action be aroused. . .[to] insure a continuously progressive

upward evolution." Immigration should be restricted to prevent "the continued propagation of defective strains in the
present population."

A year later, the United States passed the Restriction Act,
which Calvin Coolidge signed, saying "America must be kept
American." Immigration from southern and eastern Europe
was essentially eliminated until the beginning of World War
II, dooming many to the war and the Holocaust.

In 1994, in a bestselling book, *The Bell Curve*, Harvard professor Richard Herrnstein and Princeton professor Charles
Murray proved that, on the basis of IQ tests, Ashkenazic Jews
were the most intelligent people on earth. The least intelligent
were classified as "Hispanic" and "black." Herrnstein and
Murray called the phenomenon of racial intellectual inferiori-
ty "dysgenesis."

13.

In the second half of the 19th century, the Semites were the
Arabs and Jews. [And would remain so until the second half
of the 20th century when, in the wake of the Holocaust and
the rise of the state of Israel, the Arab component would
recede or disappear.] The Japhetites became the Aryans, all
non-Semitic white peoples, until Aryanism excluded the non-
Germanic groups. The case of the Hamites was more complicated. With the abolition of African slavery, which was not
replaced by the large-scale enslavement of another ethnic
group, the association of Ham and slavery ended, after three
thousand years. Science and Reason pointed to a multiple creation of mankind and a Flood that had not been universal.
How else to account for all those peoples whose territories
had now been mapped and skulls now measured: black
Africans, Australian aborigines, East Asians, South Indians,
Polynesians, American Indians? Gobineau's scientific mythology prevailed: There were the black, yellow, and red "elements" who had, in certain places, remained pure in themselves, and in others had mingled in varying degrees with the
descendants of the originally white Sons of Noah.

The Hamites became the Abyssinians (Ethiopians), thanks to John Hanning Speke in 1863 and his sensational *Journal of the Discovery of the Source of the Nile*. The Abyssinians were not only Hamites, but also "semi-Shem," for their royal family traced its lineage back to King David. This accounted for their lighter skin, taller stature, and more angular faces, compared to most sub-Saharan Africans, as well as the early conversion by many to Christianity. When Speke reached Lake Victoria and discovered a large kingdom ruled by the Wahuma or Watusi (Tutsi), who looked somewhat similar to the Abyssinians, he imagined a history of a partially white Hamite race, conquering and civilizing the dark Bantu savages. Because of his book's immense popularity, Speke's invention became standard African history.

Until 1894, when the German Count von Götzen became the first European to reach the royal court, the kingdom of Rwanda was one of the last blank spots on the African map, surrounded by mountains and guarded by a notoriously fierce army. What he found was a kind of geographical paradise of rich land, gentle hills, and a temperate climate, without the tsetse flies and malarial mosquitoes that were so prevalent beyond its natural borders. The king of the land was a Tutsi, Rwabugiri, whose family had ruled for some generations and had evolved an elaborate state mechanism.

Three peoples lived in the kingdom: the original inhabitants, the Twa, who had dwindled to a tiny minority and were potters, menial laborers in the court and, incongruously, famous as the best soldiers in the king's army; the majority Hutus, a Bantu people who were largely farmers; and the ruling Tutsis, who were mainly cattle-herders. This tripartite division was not, however, of primary importance to the Rwandans, whose society was divided into fourteen "clans" that were more political than biological, including both Hutus and Tutsis, and based on an intricate system of patronage. Although the two groups generally had dissimilar physical appearances, they lived side by side, often intermarried, spoke the same language exactly the same way, and had the same religious beliefs and stories. In certain cases, a Hutu family could, through a complex process, become Tutsi.

Along with the first Europeans came an epidemic of rinderpest that in some places killed 90% of the cattle; an outbreak of smallpox; and the first appearance of a plague of sand fleas that burrowed under the toenails and painfully festered. King Rwabugiri died in 1895, creating a political instability that turned to chaos with the arrival of Belgian troops a few months later. By 1898, the country was a German colony; recaptured by the Belgians in 1916, it was permanently awarded to them after the German defeat in World War I.

The Europeans could not understand the clan system, and could only see the Rwandans in racial terms. The Twa, according to one Belgian report, was "a member of a worn and quickly disappearing race. . . with a monkey-like flat face and a huge nose, quite similar to the apes he chases in the forest." The Hutu "display very typical Bantu features. . . . They are generally short and thick-set with a big head, a jovial expression, a wide nose, and enormous lips. They are extroverts who like to laugh and lead a simple life." The Tutsis, however, are a "good race that has nothing of the negro, apart from his color"; "his features are very fine"; the women are "slender and pretty." "Gifted with a vivacious intelligence, the Tutsi displays a refinement of feelings which is rare among primitive people. He is a naural-born leader, capable of extreme self-control and of calculated goodwill." Another report praised their "Caucasian skulls and beautiful Greek profiles." For the Europeans, these Hamites, though not quite "us," were as close as could be found in Africa.

The Belgians were active colonists, appropriating land, building roads and plantations of coffee, tea, and quinine, weakening or dismantling the clan system, forbidding the polygamy that was the basis of family structure. The Tutsis, as their "natural" allies, were given administrative and other important posts; their children were sent to schools. Hutu chiefs and other leaders were replaced by Tutsis; their children kept illiterate. Catholic missionaries converted the Tutsis, inventing a myth that they were a lost tribe of Coptic Christians. Physical characteristics, however, were not the determining attributes. In 1934, the Belgians introduced identity cards for every citizen. Any man with ten or more cattle, as well as his descendants, was Tutsi; a man with less was Hutu. A Twa was anyone "recognized as Twa."

After World War II, the Belgians switched their allegiance to the Hutus. Protestant missionaries had been converting the Hutus, alarming the Catholics, who increased their missionary presence with a large number of Flemish priests. The Flemish, themselves the powerless half of a divided country, identified with this beleaguered majority group. Furthermore, the Tutsi leaders were agitating for independence. After complicated political maneuvers, alliances, and betrayals, violence broke out in 1959. The Hutus, having been raised on the Hamite myth, considered themselves the original Rwandans, and attacked the Tutsi "invaders." Ten thousand Tutsis were killed, and many tens of thousands fled across the borders. With independence in 1962, the situation became the mirror opposite of life under Belgian rule: The remaining Tutsis were stripped of power and refused education. The system of identity cards was retained, and many Tutsis paid bribes to be turned into Hutus.

Corruption; further slaughters of Tutsis and mass exoduses; repressive dictatorships supported by the West for their anticommunism and Christian piety; assassinations; Tutsi guerrilla raids from across the borders and alliances with Hutu democratic dissidents and hostile African neighbors; the collapse of coffee prices; general unemployment; the collapse of the currency; crop failures; AIDS; a massive military build-up and training, paid and organized by the French to support the Francophone Hutus against the Tutsis who, in their generation of exile, had become Anglophone in Uganda and Tanzania; the importing of enormous numbers of machetes from China; extremist Hutu radio stations and newspapers repeating the message that the great mistake of the past was allowing the Tutsis to leave and grow strong abroad; and finally the death of President Juvenal Habyarimana on April 6, 1994, his plane shot down by missiles at the Kigali airport.

The next day began a hundred days of slaughter. Hutus of all ages, women and men from all levels of society, priests and intellectuals among them, hacked Tutsis to death with the widely distributed machetes. As physical appearance was no indication, the identity cards, still in use, determined who was Tutsi; neighbors denounced those who had false cards. Schoolteachers killed their students; children of mixed marriages killed their Tutsi parent. At least 700,000 Tutsis died, 85% of them, and a tenth of the country's entire population.

In May, some 25,000 bodies, many of them headless or mutilated, came down the Kagera River, crashing in the cataracts, dropping over the beautiful Rusomo Falls. Bodies bobbed in the pools below; dogs came to pick at them. One man from the nearest village, Kasensero—the place where AIDS began— said he saw the tumbling dead bodies of a woman with five small children tied to her arms and legs.

The Kagera River flows from Rwanda into the western edge of Lake Victoria. At its northern shore, the lake empties over the Ripon Falls into the rapids of the Victoria Nile, flows north to Lake Kyoga then west to Lake Albert, turns north again, drops over the furious Murchison Falls, is renamed the Albert Nile, barely moves through the forests, enters the Sudan, is renamed the Mountain Nile, widens, rushes through the gorges of the Fola Rapids into the swamps of the Gondokoro slopes, flows into Lake No thick with sudd, is joined by the Sobat, turns east, turns north, is renamed the White Nile, crossing the vast alluvial plains until, at Khartoum, 1,600 miles along, its gray-green waters meet the blue of the Blue Nile coming down from the highlands of Ethiopia. The Hutus believed they were sending the Children of Ham home.

[December 1999]

SOURCES & ACKNOWLEDGMENTS

Besides those sources mentioned in the text, much of the information in these essays is drawn from the following:

(African Rights), *Rwanda: Death, Despair, and Defiance.*

Charles Allen & Sharada Dwivedi, *Lives of the Indian Princes.*

Don Cameron Allen, *The Legend of Noah.*

R. D. Arkush & L.O. Lee, eds., *Land without Ghosts: Chinese Impressions of America from the Mid-Nineteenth Century to the Present.*

Joseph Berger, "Sect Ordered to Stop Sheltering Teenagers," *The New York Times,* 9 June 1985.

John Bierhorst, *Cantares Mexicanos: Songs of the Aztecs.*

Robin Blackburn, *The Making of New World Slavery.*

Alan Bold, *MacDiarmid: A Critical Biography.*

John K. Chance, *Race and Class in Colonial Oaxaca.*

Norman Cohn, *Noah's Flood.*

A .K. Coomaraswamy, *Selected Papers: Metaphysics.*

J. R. W. Coxhead, *Legends of Devon.*

Stefán Einarsson, *History of Icelandic Prose Writers 1800–1940.*

Dorothy M. Figueira, *The Exotic: A Decadent Quest.*

J. T. Fraser, N. Lawrence & F. C. Haber, eds., *Time, Science, and Society in China and the West.*

Sushil Kumar De, *History of Sanskrit Poetics.*

Dennis Dutton, ed., *The Forger's Art.*

Achilles Fang, "Lu Ki's 'Rhymeprose on Literature,'" *New Mexico Quarterly,* Autumn 1952.

Jill L. M. Furst, *The Natural History of the Soul in Ancient Mexico.*

Nancy Gish, ed., *Hugh MacDiarmid: Man and Poet.*

Duncan Glen, ed., *Hugh MacDiarmid: A Critical Survey.*

William Golant, *The Long Afternoon: British India 1601–1947.*

Daniel Goleman, "New Kind of Memory Found to Preserve Moments of Emotion," *The New York Times,* 25 October 1994.

Nicholas Goodrick-Clarke, *Hitler's Priestess: Savitri Devi, the Hindu-Aryan Myth, and Neo-Nazism.*

John Gray, *The Canaanites.*

Steven Heller, *The Swastika: A Symbol Beyond Redemption?*

S. K. Heninger, Jr., *Touches of Sweet Harmony: Pythagorean Cosmology and Renaissance Poetics.*

Viðar Hreinsson, ed., *The Complete Sagas of Icelanders.*

Daniel H. H. Ingalls, *An Anthology of Sanskrit Court Poetry.*

David Johnston, "Once-Notorious '60s Commune Evolves into Respectability; After 19 Years the Lyman Family Prospers as Craftsmen and Farmers," *Los Angeles Times,* 4 August 1985.

Jonathan Mark Kenoyer, *Ancient Cities of the Indus Valley Civilization.*

Fritz Kramer, *The Red Fez: Art and Spirit Possession in Africa.*

Bruce Lincoln, *Death, War, and Sacrifice.*

Donald S. Lopez, Jr., ed., *Curators of the Buddha.*

⎯⎯⎯⎯ , ed., *Religions of India in Practice.*

199

Thomas Lyttle, ed., *Psychedelics.*
Terence McKenna, *The Archaic Revival.*
P. J. Marshall, ed., *The British Discovery of Hinduism in the Eighteenth Century.*
Thomas R. Metcalf. *Ideologies of the Raj.*
George L. Mosse, *The Crisis of German Ideology: Intellectual Origins of the Third Reich.*
Catharine Newbury, *The Cohesion of Oppression: Clientship and Ethnicity in Rwanda 1860–1960.*
Wendy Doniger O'Flaherty, *Dreams, Illusion and Other Realities.*
_____ , ed., *Karma and Rebirth in Classical Indian Traditions.*
Emiko Ohnuki-Tierney, ed., *Culture Through Time: Anthropological Approaches.*
Stephen Owen, *Readings in Chinese Literary Thought.*
Satya S. Pachori, ed., *Sir William Jones: A Reader.*
John Paddock, ed., *Ancient Oaxaca.*
R. I. Page, *Chronicles of the Vikings.*
Peter Parker, *Ackerley.*
Benita Parry, *Delusions and Discoveries: Studies on India in the British Imagination 1880–1930.*
Bertha S. Phillpotts, trans., *The Life of the Icelander Jón Ólafsson.*
Léon Poliakov, *The Aryan Myth.*
Gérard Prunier, *The Rwanda Crisis: History of a Genocide.*
Raghunath Safaya, *Indian Psychology.*
Raymond Schwab, *The Oriental Renaissance.*
P. W. Sherman, J. U. M. Jarvis & R. D. Alexander, eds., *The Biology of the Naked Mole-Rat.*
David Shulman, "The Scent of Memory in Hindu South India," *Res* 13, Spring 1987.
B. Smith & H.B. Reynolds, eds., *The City as Sacred Center.*
J. Frank Stimson, *Songs and Tales of the Sea Kings.*
George W. Stocking, Jr., *Race, Culture, and Evolution.*
Sara Suleri, *The Rhetoric of English India.*
William H. Swatos, Jr. & Loftur Reimar Gissurarson, *Icelandic Spiritualism.*
Thomas R. Trautmann, *Aryans and British India.*
Gerardus van der Leeuw, *Sacred and Profound Beauty: The Holy in Art.*
Paul Wheatley, *The Pivot of the Four Quarters.*
David Gordon White, *Myths of the Dog-Man.*
Philip Winslow, *Sowing the Dragon's Teeth: Land Mines and the Global Legacy of War.*
Roger Wolmuth, "After Two Oft-Troubled Decades, the Lyman Family Commune Scores a Sweet Song of Success at Last," *People*, 22 September 1986.
Gordon Wright, *MacDiarmid: An Illustrated Biography.*

These essays were written, thanks, in one way or another, to Bei Dao, Peter Cole, Lydia Davis, George Evans, Forrest Gander, Herdis Gunnarsdóttir & Brooks Walker, the late James Laughlin, Aurelio Major, Margarita de Orellana & Alberto Ruy Sánchez, the late Octavio Paz, Richard Sieburth, Lee Smith, and Nathaniel Tarn.